Praise for Mike Nelson's *Stop* .... *..... Life*
(Career Press, 2001):

You understand.

Yours is the first book written by someone whom I feel understands my problem is not just disorganization or poor housekeeping skills. I've realized that it has to do with what I think I deserve. I sabotage myself at work, not doing things I know I should do, teetering on the brink of failure/success constantly. I don't think I deserve a comfortable home and financial life, so I don't allow it to happen.

Nobody outside knows. I am well-groomed, social, upbeat, 'normal'. Thank you for the work you do. You are a good person. I would love to attend a workshop. I would also be willing to start a group.—Karen.

Clutter cost me my marriage, job.

Cluttering cost me my marriage, job, self-esteem and money. Only a fellow clutterer understands the 'hold' it has on me.

Hope to meet you someday, as you write one heck of a book and I know you really know what it is like to be a clutterer.—Jean

'Accidentally' found your book.

Found your book while searching for OA literature. I have depression with anxiety disorder. I've ruined my college and work careers. I have piles of trash bags and paths to different places.

It was as if you had peered inside my journal and my home and described what you saw. Tears rolled down my face. I thought I was lazy and messy, but there is more to it. I won't let anyone into the house out of shame.

It was a blessing to find your book. I love your Website. I missed the workshop, but hope you'll return. I will be there.—Ann

Thought I'd be a clutterer 'til I died.

It was amazing the difference reading this book and going to a workshop has made in our family. I have been decluttering, but the workshop made a huge difference and brought us closer together. I felt strong, motivated, and in control. I thought I'd be a clutterer 'til I died. But not now. I know I can change.—Pam

Decluttering's like losing weight.

I liken clutter-clearing to losing weight. It can't all be done at once, you have to really desire to get started and stick with it. Not unlike losing weight, you feel better as you lose the clutter.—Sammy

You've been reading my mail!

I am 3/4 through your most excellent book and I want to know when you were here peeking in my windows.... who has been telling you about me????

*Your book arrived yesterday and I have been glued to it. How can I start uncluttering....? I'm **reading**!! You certainly have **my** number! Thank you, thank you, thank you!!*— Peggy

Heard you on Dr. Laura.

Your book is making the biggest difference ever in my life. Heard you on Dr. Laura and immediately purchased. Can't believe I missed the workshop last Feb. Will be at the next one.—Barb

Making a difference.

Wow! Perusing Clutterless.org Website, crying and laughing.—Julie

Great presenter.

It was a pleasure to meet you and to experience the workshop. You are skilled, flexible and insightful as well as entertaining.—Arlene

Caitlin Flanagan recommended *Stop Clutter From Stealing Your Life* because it "... includes a chapter on the medical view of clutter and another on how clutter can disrupt a person's sex life ...."—Atlantic Monthly

Clutter-proof Your Business

Turn Your Mess Into Success

By

MIKE NELSON

CAREER
PRESS

Franklin Lakes, NJ

CLUTTER-PROOF YOUR BUSINESS
Edited by Nicole DeFelice
Typeset by Eileen Dow Munson
Cover design by Johnson Design
Printed in the U.S.A. by Book-mart Press

To order this title, please call toll-free 1-800-CAREER-1 (NJ and Canada: 201-848-0310) to order using VISA or MasterCard, or for further information on books from Career Press.

The Career Press, Inc., 3 Tice Road, PO Box 687,
Franklin Lakes, NJ 07417
www.careerpress.com

Library of Congress Cataloging-in-Publication Data

Nelson, Mike, 1950-
    Clutter-proof your business : turn your mess into success / by Mike Nelson.
        p. cm.
    Includes bibliographical references and index.
    ISBN 1-56414-600-6 (paper)
        1. Paperwork (Office practice) I. Title.

HF5547.15 .N45 2002
651.5--dc21

2002067358

This book is dedicated to Dana,
without whom nothing would have happened.
She has done more good for those who need her
than she will ever know.

And for Toby,
who is playing Full Moon In Austin
in Heaven.

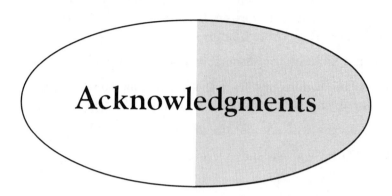

Acknowledgments

Writing may be a lonely profession, but producing a book requires the assistance of a lot of people, many of whom were strangers before a phone call or e-mail turned them into friends.

These are in no particular order of importance. Everyone is important.

- ▶ The hundreds of clutterers who talked to or e-mailed me and unknowingly offered words of encouragement just as I was doubting myself.

- ▶ The hundreds of anonymous respondents to my surveys.

- ▶ Those workshop attendees who encouraged me to keep going and shared their poignant stories.

- ▶ The workshop coordinators across the country who made my seminar series so rewarding.

- ▶ The Galveston and Houston Clutterless meeting attendees who helped keep me sane.

- ▶ Sheree Bykofsky, my agent, who started me on this path.

- ▶ Dr. Terry Early, M.D. for taking time to help me.

- ▶ Joe Nick Patoski, for his encouragement.

- ▶ Dr. Laura Schlessinger, for giving me a boost and her producer, Michelle Anton, who made the whole thing happen.

- The following busy executives who took time to answer my questions: Jimmy Rasmussen, Brian Scudamore, Gerry Coty, Ed Udelle, Rep. Craig Eiland, and Mark Farley.

- Thomas Sullivan, for his much-needed humor and feedback.

- Those anonymous tipsters in the national media who were willing to share their stories. (You know who you are).

- Tanis Evans, who put me straight on Feng Shui.

- Paul Darby, who expended a great deal of effort to educate me.

- Dana Lain, for her illustrations.

- Libby Estes, for her humor.

- Debra Duncan for giving Clutterless a big boost.

- Karen Griggs, for her most valuable insight and helpful encouragement.

- Susan, for the ADD education.

- Stacey Farkas, editor at Career Press, for putting up with me.

- Jackie Michaels, for putting effort into making the last book a success.

- K.J. McCory, for going the extra mile to introduce me to the many Professional Organizers who contributed to this project.

- Judith Kolberg, who wrote my favorite book on this subject and made me feel like I wasn't alone.

- Jan Jasper, whose book was so on-track.

- Wilma Fellman, who took a lot of time to answer questions.

- Oscar Villar, practically the only person I talked to for months, outside of interviewees.

- Joe King, for his music and pep talks that kept me at it on those 36-hour days.

- Dan McNey, for making the Dr. Laura tape.

- Eileen Byrne, whose WLS show had more impact than she could imagine.

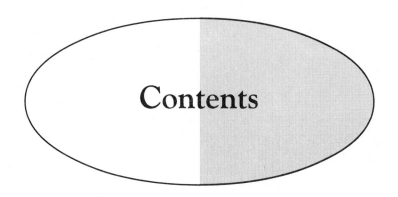

Contents

Introduction   11

Nelson's Nuggets   13

    1. What Is Really Important?   15

    2. Positive Aspects of the Way We Are   29

    3. What Kind of Clutterer Are You?   41

    4. Change Your Vocabulary, Change Your Life   53

    5. Is It AD/HD?   65

    6. What Works? What Doesn't?   71

    7. Fear Is the Enemy   83

    8. Making Decisions   93

    9. Paper Clutter and Filing Systems   107

10. Home Offices   129

11. Spiritual Is Practical   145

12. The Shadow Self   153

13. It's About Time   161

14. Go From Road Worrier to Road Warrior   169

15. Computers   179

16. Feng Shui   187

17. Is a Change in Order?   195

18. Keep It Going   203

Bibliography   209

Index   213

About the Author   219

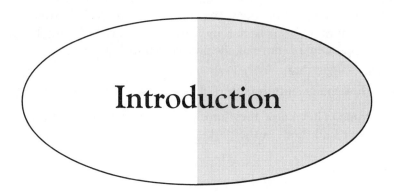

Introduction

The best review this book could get came from a clutterer. B.T. said, in response to an online survey at *www.clutterless.org*:

"All of the organizational books for work, that I've read, are written by some other type of human being. Not your average person. They all assume that it is soooo easy and if you just do as they tell you, you will NEVER have a problem again. [It] Doesn't work that way. They miss the important psychological aspects, or don't know how to address them."

Disorganization is more than piles of papers. It is an expression of a blockage in our lives, psychically, emotionally, spiritually. There is not a microwave snack of organizing tips. You'll get a seven-course dinner here, but you'll have to help prepare it. There are long-term solutions that will help us live happier, more productive, fuller lives. We'll learn to improve our lives on many levels, not just our organizing skills.

Too much organization is not the answer. It is a thief just like cluttering. Neither disorganization nor its solution is about piles of files, crowded To-Do lists, or the endless time thieves lurking in the alleys of your workaday world. It is about how you relate to those things.

Disorganization isn't about our stuff.
It's about ourselves.
The "why to" is more important than the "how to."

You'll learn how to manage your life as well as your paper piles. Your life is being sucked out of you by the clutter on your desk, in your files, and on your computer. Your social and family lives are suffering because of what is happening, or more likely, not happening, at work.

We'll change that.

Q. How many clutterers does it take to screw in a light bulb?

A. None. They know they have a dozen light bulbs, but they can't find them in the dark.

Lighten up!

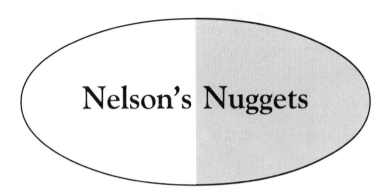

Nelson's Nuggets

For those of you "charge ahead" types, here is the meat of this book condensed into bite-sized morsels. Please don't tear the page out in the bookstore. You really will gain more understanding if you read the whole thing. But maybe you will want to refer back to these while reading, to drive home a point.

▶ Unless we work on our inner relation to our stuff, unless we identify the feelings that cause us to clutter, we are wasting our time.

▶ Information is useless unless it is available.

▶ Fear is behind cluttering.

▶ You have a special learning style. Find out if you are a visual, kinesthetic, auditory, emotional (encompassing interpersonal and intrapersonal aspects), or logical learner. Then apply that style to your work.

▶ Change your vocabulary; change your life.

▶ To get started, visualize the end.

▶ How important is it?

▶ Time spent now means time saved later.

▶ When estimating how much time you'll need for a project, give yourself an additional 10 percent and then add 20 percent for checking your work. This is the Clutterer's 80/20 rule.

▶ You are going to make mistakes. Get over them.

▶ Too tidy is too stressful.

▶ If your values are in conflict, you will be disorganized.

▶ If you are in the wrong job, you will be disorganized.

▶ Cluttering is a self-defeating behavior.

▶ There is no one solution.

▶ A cluttered desk is the sign of a cluttered mind.

▶ When overwhelmed, take a break.

▶ When overwhelmed, break the project into small tasks.

▶ Decision-making is gambling.

▶ No matter what decision you make, you will always wonder about what you didn't do.

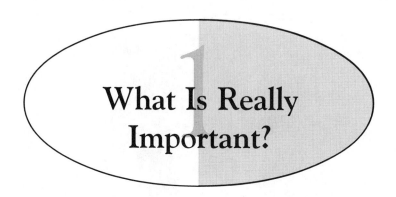

What Is Really Important?

Things do not change; we change.

—Henry David Thoreau

This book is about people, not things. Things don't clutter. We clutter. When we understand **why** we clutter, we can **permanently** change **how** we clutter. Getting our files in order is secondary to getting our life and minds in order. Whether you are mildly disorganized, overwhelmed by cluttered workspaces, or diagnosed with AD/HD, you'll benefit from these life-changing ways of approaching disorganization.

The solution is more about time-acceptance than time-management. Clutter has stolen your business; your life. A messy desk is not a sign of a genius at work or of failure. Clutter is just stuff. Your clutter is not you.

Chronic disorganization has psychological roots. Based on 879 responses to a survey on *www.clutterless.org*, 51 percent of respondents said their income was affected by cluttering, 49 percent experienced depression and 34 percent sought psychiatric counseling. Twenty nine percent of those who told their psychiatrist/psychologist about their cluttering felt it helped them to not clutter long-term. (See chart on page 16.)

At one of my seminars, a woman shouted, "I dispute your statistics!" As politely as I could, I asked her why. "I think 49 percent are depressed and 51 percent won't admit it." The audience burst into knowing laughter.

You'll learn more about letting go than controlling. The chronically disorganized try to control everything by not getting rid of anything. We waste mental energy trying to decide what to keep, what to toss, and where

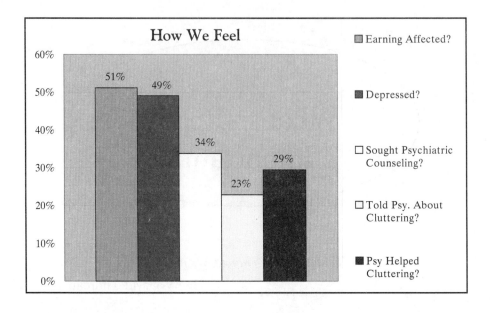

to start. We'll learn to save our energy for things that are important: our goals, our families, our friends, our creativity. We can live happier, richer lives by controlling less, but better.

A woman asked me to autograph a dog-eared, heavily highlighted copy of my last book, *Stop Clutter From Stealing Your Life.* Her story motivated me to write as if you and I were having a conversation, just two people talking about a common problem.

"You really helped me get my life back from cluttering. You seemed to understand like no one else. But it dealt with my personal life, with only a couple of chapters on business organization. When I heard you were writing a book for businesses, I had to tell you how important it would be for me, and I suspect many others.

"I've applied the principles you presented to my personal life and it really has made a difference. I'm no longer ashamed of the way I live and have friends over for the first time in years. I have a sense of serenity at home that I'd always longed for.

"Work is another story. Clutter seems like an evil Shadow Self that overwhelms me. I struggle every day just to do what seems to come to others naturally. I have difficulty making decisions, can't file things or even tell my secretary how to help me.

"I'm frequently overwhelmed. Papers come in but never go out. Everything seems equally important. I fear that if I file something, I'll forget it. It will turn out to be crucial and I'll make a serious business error. I feel like I'm just one piece of paper away from failing.

"I work 60 hours a week at the office and then part of the weekend at home. My family life suffers. I started my own business to give me more time for my family, more freedom and independence, but have found those to be hollow promises.

"In the workshop today, you said something that electrified me. 'We clutterers have replaced people in our lives with things. We can learn to put things into perspective. People are important, not things.'

"So how do I do it? I've bought business organization books, taken seminars, hired a business coach and really, really tried. They all had great ideas that apparently work for other people. I honestly tried to implement them in my business. I really did. Things were better for a few weeks, but then they fell apart again.

"I'm smart, well-educated, and motivated. I have an MBA from UCLA. But sometimes I feel like a failure. What's wrong with me? Why have I let simple things like too much paper, agonizing over decision-making, and wasting so much time trying to find things ruin my life? My company does well, but I have to work twice as hard as I should to keep it going. I feel like I'm running as fast as I can and staying in the same place. Can you please help me?"

Cluttering Is About Feelings, Not Papers

When Mary finished, there were tears in her eyes. She is an intelligent, educated businesswoman who felt inadequate, defeated by clutter. Cluttering is not about filing papers. It isn't about making better "To-Do" lists. It comes from deep inside us, a manifestation of our fears and insecurities. As Pogo said, "We have met the enemy and he is us." We've got to work on our insides before we can effectively change our outsides.

The terms "cluttering," "disorganization," "chronically disorganized," and "clutterers" are interchangeable. I don't use "packrat" or other euphemisms. Cluttering is a compulsive behavior. Cluttering is serious, but learning not to take ourselves so seriously is part of getting over it. Lighten up and defuse clutter's hold on you. This isn't a tome. You'll laugh out loud as you identify with other clutterers.

Cluttering is a psychological and spiritual blockage in our lives that hampers our job performance, steals time from our families, and fosters feelings of inadequacy in people who are far from inadequate. Cluttering is seldom life-threatening, but it does cause accidents at work and home.

How to Be Organized for the Long-Term

1. Before you start an organizing project, visualize the results.

2. Make small, concrete goals like eliminating an inch of paper or clearing a square foot of desk.

3. Get a "Clutter Buddy" to help you. Making a commitment to a nonjudgmental person works wonders.

4. Learn your learning style and apply it to your office.

5. Learn how to make decisions so they don't overwhelm you.

6. Learn how you relate to time and make it work for you.

7. Create a backup filing system, like training wheels on a bicycle, to get started.

8. Before filing anything, say "HI" to it—"How Important Is It?"

9. Use your computer to eliminate paper files.

10. Incorporate your life-goals with what you do with your life.

11. Believe in yourself.

12. Make friends with your Shadow Self.

13. Learn to meditate.

14. Channel your rebellion.

15. You may have to create a new job to be happy.

Improve Your Memory—Right Now!

We don't have bad memories. We just don't know how to use them. You can start right now and get more from reading.

Your dog remembers what is important better than you. Admittedly, dogs have fewer things on their minds than most of us, but they do know

I wanna focus...
I really wanna focus...
pant, pant, pant.

what is important. They know because they focus. A god's, er dog's, focus is you. He knows you are important to his goals of eating, sleeping in a comfortable place, and being loved. While you may never be as smart as your dog, you can learn to focus and your memory will improve dramatically.

We remember better when we are actively involved.

As you read, ask yourself two questions:

1. "What's he going to say next?"

2. "How does this apply to me?"

That's it! Just doing those two things will make the process more personal; more memorable. Use your dominant senses. Scribble in the margins. Visualize what you read. Read out loud if you are an auditory learner.

Fear and Feeling Overwhelmed Are the Enemies

Between 80 and 90 percent of the information we save has no real value. Surveys show that average Americans spend **an entire year** of their working lives searching through desk clutter or looking for misplaced objects. Executives waste up to **six weeks** a year looking for misfiled or mislabeled papers.

You are overwhelmed by paper. You are overwhelmed by time. You save useless papers because of fear of making a mistake. You are afraid that, if you discard something, it will come in useful later. You are afraid that we will lose our jobs if we don't CYA. Stop letting fear run, and ruin, your business. Let's set some intelligent, practical guidelines for making decisions and empowering you and your employees to make good decisions.

Journalists Are in a Category of Their Own

If anyone should know how little value old information has, it would be journalists. Yet, many of them admitted (in a whisper to me) that they were office clutterers. Not one wanted to be identified, out of a fear of being found out, or shame. They **know** that the stories they've written or taped are dated minutes after they do them. They have libraries or morgues (which should tell you something about how they feel about old news) for research. Their Internet and computer storage abilities dwarf yours and mine.

They keep old newspapers, video and audio tapes, books and magazines around, in, and on top of their desks like skinny squirrels preparing for a hard winter. These clutter-caches are organized archeologically, if at all. Indexed? What's that?

I was in the office of a major national newspaper helping one editor with his clutter. We made some progress and he assured me he would keep it up. I didn't say anything, but I know it takes more than one attempt to overcome this habit. I called him a few months later and, sure enough, he was foraging for information again.

Q. "Is it fair to say newspaper reporters are cluttered at work?"

A. (Preceded by a large laugh) **"Yes, absolutely."**

Q. "Why?"

A. "Because we are so often on deadlines and we get such mountains of information on paper. It's surprising, since we get so much e-mail."

Q. "What **has** worked for you?"

A. "That two-day rule you suggested worked best for a while."
(If you haven't read something in two days, dump it. That's harsher than I usually am with a clutterer, but it seemed like it would fit in with the newspaperman's logic).
Then I tried to keep a small area of the desk clear and "sacred." Just a small area. It did make me more mindful of stuff to toss. But that was temporary, too.

Q. "Do you think fear of making a mistake is behind it all?"

A. "No. It is fear of not knowing something I should know about."

That was the answer I got almost verbatim from everyone I talked to. Hanging onto stuff is based in insecurity—even when a person is secure in his job and personal life. Fear of one kind or another is the basis of our cluttering.

Radio people aren't immune. I've known radio personalities who have multiple copies of shows they've done in moldy cardboard boxes. There's no indexing, but there's comfort in knowing they are there—somewhere.

Another nationally known anonymous tipster shared this with me:

"Broadcast entities have to keep their copy for a certain length of time by law. So yes, there is clutter.

"I remember working at a station where the news director kept every newspaper for three years. He used it as his reference file.

"Another station where I worked had so many files that they were stacked along the inner halls of the office, alongside each cubicle some four feet high. That station has now moved to a larger office with approximately the same number of workers.

"At yet another station, I found files of copy dating back 10 years. Quite a feat considering it was a town that had the occasional shooting, accident, and small town news that really shouldn't have filled more than a couple of file boxes."

And so it goes. Who'd 'a' thunk it?

Before and After

HOW WE FEEL BECAUSE OF OUR DISORGANIZATION	
NOW WE FEEL	WE'LL LEARN TO FEEL
Overwhelmed.	Control.
Chaos.	Order.
Friction.	Harmony.
Fearful.	Confident.
Confused.	Serene.

Do you identify with the feelings in the left-hand column? We live in chaos at work and home. Clutter creates friction with our bosses, co-workers, and clients. It affects our relationships with our families. We are afraid of making mistakes, losing our jobs, hurting our businesses because of our disorganization. Our mental clutter keeps us in a state of confusion.

Now the bright side: the right side. We **can control** our cluttering behaviors. When we clutter less, we experience order and harmony in our lives. We trust ourselves to make decisions and regain confidence in ourselves. **Clarity replaces confusion.**

My Promises to You

If you get the sudden inspiration that you are "cured," feel free to jump up and shout, "Hallelujah! Brother Nelson has cured me!" and go forth to clutter no more. I wish I could promise you that, by the time you finish reading, you will be permanently organized. It will get you started, but it took you years to get where you are today. It will take time to be clutter-free. **Your organization will improve right away**. But, you will have to work at not-cluttering (kind of a Zen concept) for the rest of your life. The longer you do it, the easier it gets. After awhile, you'll wonder how you ever lived the way you are now.

Radical Changes Ahead

People are disorganized for a reason. Imposing systems and organizing tips on yourself or your employees, without addressing the root of the problem is like applying a bandage to cover a broken arm. It looks better for awhile, but doesn't solved the underlying problem. You'll end up with employees who ignore the new systems because they have not changed their beliefs. Together, we will help clutter-junkies wean themselves off their addiction to C.H.A.O.S. (Change Hurts And Organizing Stinks) and bring them back to being the effective employees they want to be.

You may have hired an organizational coach, professional organizer, or Feng Shui Master who set you up with great systems. You learned about "zones" and "homes" and how to "handle each piece of paper only once." Six months later, some of your employees are organized and others are as bad as ever. Why?

The organizers and coaches I interviewed are professionals who know what works for most people. Their ideas are sound. Their systems are good. I've combined their conventional methods with new ideas that will help the chronically disorganized.

Sometimes the solutions are as simple as adapting filing systems and time-management to a person's dominant learning modality. Visual people need more colors or they feel trapped in a manila jungle. Kinesthetic people need to "touch" what they are doing. Auditory people can incorporate sound into office routines. Those with AD/HD can utilize their strengths by changing the way they do things. Sometimes, the reasons are rooted in psychology. Psychologists tell us that we do not do things unless we get a payoff from them. The payoff can be negative or positive, but there is a payoff to every action—or inaction.

Organizing Is Like Going on a Diet

Organizing books are a lot like dieting books. It is estimated about half of Americans are on some form of diet on any given day. We need organizing books just as we need dieting books because we are a bloated, overweight society, in terms of information clutter and physical body mass. Oddly enough, a related benefit to decluttering is weight-loss. Presented properly, this could be a great motivator. Maybe your new motto could read, "Cut the fat—corporate and personal."

Anyone who's been on a diet will agree that unless we change our fundamental relationship with food, we won't lose weight. Unless we change our fundamental relationship with our stuff, we won't get organized. Not everyone needs to be model-slim or over-organized. It could be that you are a square peg trying to fit into a round hole and a change of position is in order.

Too Tidy Is Too Stressful

Clutterers are uncomfortable keeping picture-perfect desks, immaculate, sparse files. The effort of doing this causes them more stress that their mess did. **Not everyone who is a little disorganized is a clutterer**. It's only when your disorganization gets in the way of your life and your way of living that it's a problem. Some of these practical suggestions about using your learning style may be all you need. You don't need the in-depth understanding that a real clutterer needs to be productive. Take what you need and leave the rest.

Joe Nick Patoski is a senior editor for *Texas Monthly* Magazine. His office would never win any awards from *Office Beautiful* Magazine, but he functions perfectly in his world. He is a hard worker, steady producer, and writes extensively—books, articles, and interviews. He admits to being cluttered at his home office. "I'm probably not going to do much about it. It works for me. My work is my priority. How I do it is secondary."

Use Your Senses

Anthony Robbins (*Unlimited Power, Awaken The Giant Within*) encourages us to determine what senses we use to learn best. We have five senses, but few of us can learn organization through taste or smell (although most people will agree that being disorganized stinks). According to my survey and interviews, the majority of clutterers learn kinesthetically—by doing.

People can tell us how to do something, but unless we actively touch and do, it won't last. That's why a clutterer has to clean his own files, or clear her own desk. If someone does it for us, it isn't real.

Decluttering Is Boring

> "I do the work of 10 women during the day. Yet, my files are a mess, my desk is a mess. It hampers me, but I don't do anything about it because, decluttering it is, well, boring."
>
>   —Joan at a Clutterless meeting.

Clutterers generally have a great, if wry, sense of humor. They lose interest if something is humorless. (One of the memory techniques you'll learn is to attach humor to those things we need to remember). That's another reason we have a hard time decluttering. It is boring. It's hard to find humor in an inbox of old faxes. So, we'll learn to make a game of decluttering. Perhaps one day we'll have decluttering Olympics.

Who We Are—The Short Version

Most clutterers are intuitive thinkers. Unfortunately, we have deluded ourselves into believing that we are logical. Mr. Spock, we ain't. Our systems have an illogic to them that makes sense to us. Joe Nick again, "What you see as clutter I see as a semblance of order."

We are generally creative. We like to paint big mental pictures. Then we get lost in the minutiae. We start out wanting to be Rembrandts and end being poor imitations of Salvador Dali or Picasso. We love projects. We just aren't crazy about finishing them.

Our clutter is inherently visual, but we don't see it the same way as a non-clutterer. Where an organized person sees a mess, we see a system. Like a little boy digging through a pile of manure, we're sure there's a pony in there somewhere. We would make great treasure hunters (except for keeping track of the details like where we'd already searched and how much air we had left in our Scuba tanks). I gave up Scuba diving after going through all the trouble to get certified. There were just too many details. I'd rather fish. It's simpler. Bait a hook, throw it in, and wait. A clutterer has a hard time remembering to do more than three things at a time.

Our mental clutter never stops. (AD/HD people know exactly what I'm talking about). Sometimes it's nagging voices in our heads, reminding us of all the things we haven't done. Sometimes it's just white noise. Some of us even carry visual representation of everything that bothers us in our heads. One of our goals is to quiet our minds and stop the voices or images so that we can get to work on the problem.

Is It AD/HD?

Clutterers often ask if cluttering is related to AD/HD (Attention Deficit Disorder). The only way to know if you have AD/HD is to be diagnosed by physician, but the short answer is, it is statistically unlikely. According to the Attention Deficit Disorder Association (*www.add.org*), "Approximately four percent to six percent of the U.S. population has ADHD." (Dr. Kathleen G. Nadeau PhD, author of *AD/HD in the Workplace*, says it could be as high as 10 percent.) We often have AD/HD-like tendencies, but so do most people. When we learn not to clutter, these tendencies improve. According to the ADDA, "The 'official' clinical diagnosis is Attention Deficit Hyperactivity Disorder, or AD/HD." The term 'ADD' is commonly used by the general public, those with the disorder, and to describe the condition without the hyperactivity component.

Clutterers also wonder if they are hoarders (an obsessive-compulsive disorder). About one percent of the population hoards. Because of the publicity given these conditions, they are the only labels we know. Labeling can be a first step to identifying something that can be treated. But it's not an excuse. Saying, "I have AD/HD, so you can't expect me to be organized," is not acceptable, as anyone who works with AD/HD patients will tell you.

There are many successful and productive people who have AD/HD. They've learned how to use their unique way of looking at things to their advantage. You can too. Being a clutterer means you have a different way of viewing the world. We are going to teach you to turn those "liabilities" into assets. You are not "bad." You are not "hopelessly disorganized." You just don't learn the same way as other people or respond to "traditional" organizing techniques.

But I Gotta Give It a Name

Call yourself a clutterer. It's not a medical diagnosis. It isn't an excuse for your behavior. But it does give you a name to your condition. That helps a lot, as anyone with any condition that wasn't identified years ago will tell you. In our grandparents' day, people were diagnosed as suffering from "brain fever," or "the vapors." We can do better than that, now. You aren't alone. There are many millions of us. We just haven't had a name, to identify ourselves. We do have a national support group, Clutterless Recovery Groups, Inc. (*www.clutterless.org*), but we are mostly in our Fibber McGee closets about our condition. For those who are too young to remember this popular radio show, Fibber McGee and Molly had a hall closet so full of stuff that whenever he opened it, cascading possessions rained down on him. He always meant to declutter his closet, "one of these days," but never got around to it.

How Do I Know So Much About This?

I call myself a "reformed clutterer." That means I am much better now than I was a few years ago. I still clutter to some extent and always will. I can almost always find what I'm looking for. I don't live in chaos. Life is good and constantly getting better. You'll say the same things when we're finished.

The destination is not a minimalist, super-neat office. It is an office where I can be productive, find things when I need them and still express my individuality. I am not happy in minimalist surroundings. **Too tidy is too stressful**.

My last job

In my last "real" job, I started out as a staff writer, ending up as vice-president in charge of publishing for an international corporation that published guidebooks. Typical for a clutterer, I over committed and wrote a weekly column for some small newspapers.

Fortunately for all of us, 40 percent of my job meant being on the road for a month or more at a time. I drove a van packed with: a portable bathtub Jacuzzi, several suitcases, three camera bags, books, tools, various knick-knacks, and a human assistant.

The office ran quite smoothly without me. At first, I held the largest office in the back, with oak-paneled walls and a door. My old office was littered with loose papers, had five filing cabinets, and housed hundreds of books. No one could see my mess. When the company needed the big office for two new employees. I was shuttled to a glass cubicle. I crammed all that stuff into half the space. I justified my tower of clutter because I needed the information "for research." Management put up a partition so my mess wouldn't distract everyone else. My boss said it gave him a headache just glancing in there.

Quiet, genius at work

A newspaper editor told me, "A disorganized genius could get away with a lot. The rest of us have to fit in." I passed myself off as a genius.

Shallow goals

Being "famous" was my life-goal. I achieved it, but, like all illusory goals (a big house, fancy cars, etc.) it wasn't as satisfying as I thought it would be. I got fan mail. *The New York Times, The Wall Street Journal, Texas Monthly,* and many others wrote stories about me. I met the reporters in Mexico to keep them away from my office. A Mexican reporter sneaked up on us one day. He couldn't take a picture of me at my desk because the piles of books, papers, and God-knows-what hid me. Now I know that we hide behind our clutter, literally and figuratively.

Failure to Success

I made many attempts to "get organized." They all worked for a short time, but ultimately failed. Honestly, I didn't think I could change my habits. I thought that was just the way I was. New management came in and began their decluttering with me. I was on the street.

The full story is in my last book, but the short version is that after a fiancé divined that I loved my junk more than I loved her, I got help from a support group. So far, I've eliminated over a ton-and-a-half of clutter from my homes and home offices, been free enough to move four times in three years, and now live and work in two rooms. Sometimes my office is messier than I'd like (like right now, while I am in the middle of a big project), but it is **never** even close to what it was like four years ago. How neat is it? I could go back to that glass cubicle if I wanted to and no one would be ashamed to have me there. But I don't want to.

What Is Really Important?

Decluttering has taught me that my Really Big Goals are freedom and helping others. "Being famous" was hollow, fleeting, and self-indulgent. Getting rid of the excess stuff, and the disorganization that came with it, was the first step on a road to self-discovery. I've since talked to thousands of clutterers. They are amazed when they discover how decluttering opens up their lives. They get more out of life when they learn that less, is indeed, more.

Become a Cartographer

You'll get far more than organizing tips here. You'll learn how to create a master map to whatever and wherever your Really Big Goals are. You'll learn how to organize your files, handle mail and papers expeditiously, and more mundane things, but that's incidental. You'll learn to make decisions and feel more self-confident. You'll learn how to organize your life and clear the clutter from your mind, heart, and soul. You will see a whole new path open to you that has been blocked by your physical, mental, and emotional clutter. That's a pretty good deal for the investment of less than 20 bucks, don't you think?

Positive Aspects of the Way We Are

*My lack of obsession about organization has made
me more adaptable to temporary chaos. I am more
adaptable to and forgiving of chaos that is less preventable,
such as natural disaster. I am less patient with chaos
resulting from poor planning or lack of communication.*

—Martha, a manager of a large telecommunications firm

You've been browbeaten about your disorganization enough. You've probably been made to feel bad about it by co-workers, bosses, mates, and friends. You may feel like a "bad" person or a failure. You're not. You do what you do because there are certain benefits, or payoffs, to it. Before we can talk about changing those behaviors, we have to be honest with ourselves about them. We're not talking about a "quick fix" here; we're talking about changing a lifetime of habits.

More than 20 years ago, a psychiatrist said something to me that helped me understand this. I went to him because I wanted to stop drinking. Rather than patting me on the back and saying, "Good for you." He reflected for a moment and asked me, "why?"

I'd read a lot of self-help books and knew the correct answer. "I'm ready to change a negative behavior."

"Why?" he asked again. (I think that's the first word they learn in psychiatry school).

"Because drinking has caused nothing but bad consequences for me," I said, still feeling like I was being a good pupil.

"How long have you been drinking?"

"Since I was 14."

"So, you mean to tell me that in 18 years of drinking, not one good thing ever happened to you?"

"Well, of course it did, Doc. But the cumulative effect was bad."

"People generally don't do something for a long period of time unless they derive some benefit from it. When we deny part of what we want to change, we are trying to suppress it. In order to achieve self-determination, we have to be honest. We acknowledge both the good and the bad."

"But Doc, isn't drinking a bad thing?"

"Not necessarily. Plenty of people drink socially and suffer no ill consequences. Many people drink too much occasionally and don't drive drunk, don't lose their spouses or their careers. Would you say drinking is bad for them?"

"Uh, no I guess not. But what about me?"

"That's what we're here to find out. We're here to find out about you. What is it about drinking and you that is the problem?"

Social Clutterers and Chronic Clutterers

Most people are sometimes disorganized. Normally organized people can have a messy desk or overcrowded filing cabinets and miss appointments from time to time. They see that the payoff of being disorganized is negative, and take steps to correct it. I'd call them social clutterers.

People like us however, don't have the self-awareness we need to nip the problem in the bud. In fact, even though we feel like we ought to change (so we buy books like this one), we hold onto the idea that it really isn't that bad. We can justify our behavior by citing the many times being disorganized has actually been a good thing.

Sound Familiar?

Here are some statements people have made in defense of staying cluttered:

"I cleaned out my filing cabinet and, sure enough, I threw away a file I needed just a week later."

"I threw away a box of old receipts and got audited by the IRS. If I hadn't done that, I could have proved my deductions."

"I got rid of a lot of old books in my library and later saw one of them selling at a used bookstore for $750."

"I kept putting off the start of a project at work and sure enough, we lost the contract before it was even due. If I had been completely organized, I would have wasted a lot of time."

"I couldn't find a client's phone number, so I didn't call him back. The next week, he declared bankruptcy. If I'd been organized, and taken his order, I'd be out a lot of money."

I'm sure you can think of some of your own stories from personal experience. They would seem to argue against doing anything about our disorganization. After all, if we hold onto everything, we will never make a mistake. Lots of situations take care of themselves. We can always justify our inaction by the old adage, "Not making a decision is a decision."

POSITIVE ASPECTS OF A CLUTTERER PERSONALITY

▶ Spontaneous.

▶ Creates excitement on job.

▶ Feeling of freedom.

▶ A "character" at work.

▶ Helpful to others.

▶ Perfectionist.

▶ Creative.

▶ Not bound by "clock time."

▶ Visually oriented.

▶ "Feeling" personality.

▶ Can ask others for help.

▶ Willing to put in long hours.

Don't Worry. You Won't Catch the Neat-Freak Disease.

See, you aren't "bad," you are creative, spontaneous, and various other good things. You may even have one of those signs on your desk proclaiming, "Genius at work," or "A messy desk is the sign of a creative mind." You might even have cartoons taped on your computer.

These positive traits are gifts. Your neat, organized friends may wish they were more spontaneous and creative. They have to work at what comes naturally to you. Those who are the hardest on you are probably afraid of their Shadow Selves, which are their disorganized selves. The goal is not to become an obsessive-compulsive straighten-upper, or robot who never leaves a file out. To us, they seem like rather joyless people.

A seminar participant in Dallas asked, "If I walked into your office, would I be overwhelmed by neatness? Are you going to turn us into neat-nuts?"

I laughed. "No, my office is usually tidy, but like all clutterers, I like to have more stuff around me and a certain amount of controlled disorder, to be happy and function well. Sometimes, even after four years of working on this issue, it gets downright sloppy."

"You mean there's no cure?"

"Being a clutterer is like having hay fever. Sometimes there's too much pollen in the air and we sneeze despite our antihistamines. We know the air will clear and the number of days we aren't overwhelmed by pollen outnumber the days when we are."

A Holistic Approach

What we are going to do on this journey is to channel those positive traits into positive directions. The traits are good, and make for interesting people. We're going to apply a holistic approach to disorganization. Holistic practitioners believe that physical symptoms in one part of the body may be related to other things going on inside. Their advice for returning to full health often involves working with things in our outer world. Their prescriptions are gentle and may contain elements of the very illness we are fighting. Dr. Dean Edell, who is one of my favorite talk-show hosts, considers the idea ludicrous from a medical standpoint. Bear with me, Dr. Dean, we're speaking philosophically here.

Some approaches to organizing are more like Western medicine. They prescribe a massive dose of antibiotics to kill (deny) the offending organism. Other than bed rest, very little is required of us. The germs get killed, and we are all better. But somehow, some germs survive and become immune to those killer antibiotics, so drug companies are continually developing new ones to fight resistant strands. We get sick again and the cycle repeats itself. Psychiatrists tell us that which we deny will break out in other areas of our personality.

We're going to use both analogies. We're going to learn some rules (antibiotics) and some behavior modification (holistic approach) to fight our disorganization. We're going to turn those very positive traits of cluttering to natural antibiotics that will keep us working healthily for the rest of our lives. That's not to say we won't get sick again, but we won't get *as* sick and will be able to deal with it alone.

Let's Look at Those Traits Again

CLUTTERING TRAITS GONE AWRY	
POSITIVE TRAIT	NEGATIVE CONNOTATIONS
Spontaneous.	Can't commit or follow a plan.
Creates excitement.	Easily bored.
Feeling of freedom.	Actually less free because of fears.
A "character."	A "slob."
Helpful.	A sap to dump work on.
Perfectionist.	Can't finish anything.
Not bound by "clock time."	Always late.
Visually oriented.	Keeps everything in sight. A mess.
"Feeling" personality.	Too emotional.
Can ask others for help.	Needy.

What we see as positive character assets are seen by others as character defects. And they are right. We've done it to ourselves. We've taken our very strengths and made them into weaknesses. We didn't do it on purpose. I haven't met anyone yet who woke up one morning and said, "I think I'm going to clutter today." I don't know one person whose goal in life was to become a clutterer.

But, all of them agreed that the positive traits in the first chart were worth developing. They were surprised when I pointed out that they already had them. That makes them successes! They developed those traits, though they don't give themselves credit for having done so.

We hear the negative comments from others about the traits in the second chart and define ourselves by them. The more we repeat an idea, the more power it has. We have given all of the power to the negative, robbing the positive.

So let's try to take our positive qualities and see where they could benefit us in the workplace.

GOOD USE OF OUR TRAITS	
POSITIVE TRAIT	BEST USE
Spontaneous.	Come up with new ideas.
Creates excitement.	Work is exciting. Impart that excitement to clients, co-workers.
Feeling of freedom.	Complete a task on time, then award yourself some little freedom like taking a walk, going to a movie, reading a book, or napping.
A "character."	Let your real personality shine through, once clutter has diminished. Be a character, not a caricature of a messy person.
Helpful.	Learn to say no. Use this by helping those who really need our skills.
Perfectionist.	Let this one go until you know how to use it.
Not bound by "clock time."	Be early. Using the "about" method of time keeping, you can have extra time to get ahead.
Visually oriented.	Place emotionally pleasing pictures on your cubicle or walls instead of sticky notes. On your desk, make your "tickler" file shine with colors.
"Feeling" personality.	Intuit what is right or wrong with a project long before the logical thinkers get it.
Can ask others for help.	People are honored to be made to feel like experts. Limit your asking to those times you really need help so you won't be a bother.
Willing to put in long hours.	Don't need to because you are organized.

Spontaneous	Come up with new ideas.

Got an idea? Put it down on paper or tell it to someone. This releases the spontaneous need you have and may help your business do things better. Clutterers (and entrepreneurs) are better at coming up with ideas than implementing them, so why not share them with someone whose strengths lie in that direction?

Creates excitement	Work is exciting. Impart that excitement to clients, co-workers.

One excuse for not organizing is that it is boring. When we dig frantically through piles of files, the search is exciting. We like the drama. When we've improved our self-esteem by being more organized, we'll channel this energy into our work.

> "One of the ways I can keep enthused and keep going is by getting rid of my clutter."
>
> —Tom Sullivan, manager of an insurance company.

I called two Galveston bookstores to find a book. A bored voice (there may have been a person behind it, but it was hard to tell) told me in a monotone, "Hello, this is _____, your book superstore. How may I direct your call?" Did that make me want to run down there and buy from them? Of course not. My next call was to a locally owned store, "Hi! This is Midsummer Books, Jay speaking. How can I help you?" Guess where I went?

Jay finds his job exciting and it shows. You may be the only contact someone has with your company. We can even learn to apply excitement to organizing (trust me on this one). If you love your job, let people know. It will help in all ways, including not cluttering. If you don't, it will show in disorganized behavior.

Your job is like your house. "I recently had houseguests. They were nice enough people, but they left their clothes and shoes all over the place. I got really angry. It was like they didn't respect my house, or by extension, me," Dan, a workshop attendee said, You'll eventually look at cluttering as disrespectful to yourself.

Feeling of freedom	Complete a task on time, then award some little freedom like taking a walk, going to a movie, reading a book, or napping.

As you learn to live less cluttered, you'll get more done in less time. Reward yourself with the thing you crave most—freedom. We've gotten things backwards up until now. We've rebelled against organizing, believing we are free spirits and that organizing would hamper our individuality. Once we create a system for ourselves, we are truly free.

A "character"   Let your real personality shine through once clutter has diminished. Be a character, not a *caricature* of a messy person.

Come on, you can admit it to me. You *like* the attention that being cluttered has gotten you. You've probably got a nickname (even if you don't know it) of "Messy Melinda" or "Mr. I Can't Find It." None of us wants to be ignored. We want others to notice us and give us strokes. Since our self-image is low, we think negative strokes are the best we can do. By learning how to better work and live, our self-image rises and our true personalities shine through. You've been an office joke, a cartoon character. Now you can show people who you really are and not be afraid.

Helpful   Learn to say no. Do this by helping those who really need our skills.

Clutterers are often the ones others come to when they need help or a volunteer for a committee at work or church. ("If you need something done, ask a busy person.") We so often crave

attention from others that we are afraid to say "No." Even if it means our own work suffers, we help others. Oddly, we do better, faster, jobs for them than we do for ourselves. That should tell us something—we **can** do things more efficiently if we really want to.

A lady once told me with tears in her eyes, "I'm afraid if I say 'no' that no one will ever call me again. No one will need my help. That means that no one will need me. I will be alone."

I used to say that those people weren't your friends anyway, so dump them. I was wrong to be so harsh. If people ask for your help too frequently, say you just don't have that information or time to do it right now. Don't make it permanent. If you gently send them away, you'll learn if they are friends or users. As your self-confidence grows, you can decide if helping them is a one-way street. If they're just using you, eliminate them from your life. Dave, a Clutterless meeting attendee told me, "I volunteered for every committee at work and church. Coworkers constantly asked me to help them with their projects. One day, I realized that I was spending all my time doing for others and had no time for my family. The amazing thing was, after I said "No," the church didn't fall apart, the company kept going, and no one hated me. That was the root of my volunteerism. I wanted to be liked."

If you had begun by denying everyone and everything that took your time, you would have gotten a reputation as unapproachable. Then the prophesy of no one needing you might have come true.

Be gentle with yourself. Don't make drastic changes overnight. Your habits are like old shoes. You've formed them around you until they are comfortable. When you get a new pair of shoes, you don't start out running marathons in them. You work up to it. So you will work up to this new way of life. If it hurts too much to change one thing, stop it! There are plenty of other habits you can work on. Pick the ones that are not as emotionally charged first.

Perfectionist   Let this one go until we know how to use it.

Misplaced perfectionism is our biggest enemy. It's often expressed in another "P" word—procrastination. We can spend hours on a small project that is only worth 15 minutes. We delay filing, completing projects, doing just about anything at all because we want it to be perfect. Making decisions is like gambling. We have to know when to stop betting, when to call, and when to draw.

When I was a stock options trader, the hardest thing to know was "when to pull the trigger." No matter when I decided to buy or sell, there was always more information, more analysis that I could have used to delay a decision. Buying at exactly the low and selling at exactly the high of the day is pure chance. The best you can do is get as close as you can. So it is with all of your work. You do the best you can with what you have and move on.

Not bound by "clock time"   Be early. Using the "about" method of
                             time keeping, you can have extra time to
                             get ahead.

If you are a clutterer who doesn't generally run late, or feel a lot of stress when having to meet deadlines (we'll change that to "finish lines" by the time we are through), then you are the first. We seem to work by a clock in our head that has more minutes in an hour than anyone else's. We can turn that to our advantage by **using** our sense of time instead of **abusing** it. Chapter 13 will give you a new way of looking at time. Ralph Keyes, author of *Timelock* (Harper Collins, 1991) and *Whoever Makes The Most Mistakes Wins: The Paradox of Innovation* (Richard Farson and Ralph Keyes, The Free Press / Simon & Schuster, June 2002) said, "One reason we love vacations (assuming our need for speed isn't chronic) and find post-vacation reentry so difficult is that once we 'lose track of time' our bodies revert to a more normal rhythm. Our nervous systems tell us in no uncertain terms how much they prefer this tempo."

Clutterers view time as the enemy. It isn't—it's just foreign to us. We can learn to use our internal clock by making appointments and "finish lines" more elastic. Instead of scheduling something at 9:15 a.m., make it at "about 8:30." We don't use a specific number of minutes or days to add to something, because we'd soon learn to outsmart ourselves. Instead, we round things to the next lower unit of time that makes sense. Kids today tell time by digital watches and tell time in exact minutes. We grew up with a round clock and were lucky to tell time within a quarter of an hour.

When we change our perception of time, we become more natural and relaxed about it. We are more likely to arrive early than late and have time that truly belongs to ourselves. That is a key issue. We have learned to resent time because it is someone else's. We **will learn** to take back our time—on our own less stressful terms.

Visually oriented	Place emotionally pleasing pictures on your cubicle or walls instead of sticky notes. On your desk, make your "tickler" file shine with colors.

A big reason we don't file things away is based on the fear that once it is out of sight, it will be out of mind.

Marita Adair, a freelance editor and former author of the *Frommer's Guides to Mexico,* uses wire baskets and see-through filing containers. She put it this way, "Make use of space. Space is part of the cluttering problem. I use under-shelf baskets—avoids wasted space. I use plastic crates as book and file dividers. They are then used as book dividers on my shelves. Literature containers help for magazines. I can organize my clutter better. I mark on my daily calendar to put away 12 things. I often do much more. When I worked in an office, I could declutter at the end of the day. In a home office everything is so fluid."

Eventually, we will begin to appreciate the blank spaces on our desks and walls as much as the items we truly need to see. Instead of a wall of project charts and a desk papered with sticky notes, we'll have beautiful things in our offices or cubicles. Beauty begets harmony. Harmony cannot coexist with clutter.

| "Feeling" personality. | Intuit what is right or wrong with a project long before the logical thinkers get it. |

Clutterers attach "stories" to things in their homes, which makes it hard to throw anything out. At work, we don't discard things for different emotional reasons, usually fear that we will make a mistake. We sense that things have more value than they do. At first, you will have to tone down that sixth sense, but as you learn to make decisions on what is important and what is not, you can learn to trust it. We can learn to trust that sixth sense as part of our creative nature. At the beginning of this chapter, there were several examples of procrastination having had its rewards. Sometimes it wasn't procrastination at all—it was your intuitive sense that told you not to do something. **You will learn to tell the difference.** Then, you can trust your unique intuition.

| Can ask others for help. | People are honored to be made to feel like experts. Limit your asking to those times you really need it, so you won't be a bother. |

Do you now seem to run out of time to finish a project and go frantically searching for a workmate who can help you meet a finish line (deadline to those of you who haven't changed your way of thinking yet)? Does this happen often?

People don't like being imposed upon, but are happy to help occasionally. If you've worn out all the welcome mats in your office, you'll learn to give everyone new ones. The fact that you are willing to ask for help is a good sign. When you are able to discern when you really need help and aren't living crisis to crisis, you won't need it so much. We are going to put **you** back in charge, not your clutter.

Willing to put in long hours. Don't need to because you are organized.

Changing our disorganized habits and eliminating the payoffs will buy us freedom. If you are spending long hours at your job because you love what you do, that is one thing. If you are spending too much time at work because you can't find what you need when you need it, that can change.

If I'm So Good, Why Do I Feel So Bad?

Gosh, you might be saying, if my traits are so good, how come I feel so bad? The answer, my friend, is because you haven't learned how to use your strengths yet. You are still op-

erating from the combined traits table, believing that the way you are is "bad." You're not bad. You're not alone, either. A self-help group like "Clutterless Recovery Groups" (*www.clutterless.org*) can offer tremendous support. The groups are not 12-Step, are nonprofit, and do offer clutterers a chance to share how their cluttering is affecting them and what they have done about it. It might be the first time you could talk about your disorganization with others who won't judge you or belittle you. They are just like you, trying to find ways to live fuller lives.

We are going to apply some practical techniques to handle the mechanics of organizing and some inner techniques to keep us on the right track.

What Kind of Clutterer Are You?

I believe anyone of sound mind can be organized.
I think different people need different kinds of help.
One person can read a book and pull himself up.
Someone else needs a cheerleader.
Another needs a leader and someone else a teacher.

—Linda Durham, owner of Organizing Matters, an
Organization Consultant and member of then
National Association of Professional Organizers

I can hear some of you snickering, saying, "Sound mind? I wouldn't know one if it bit me." Just read on, and for the moment suspend your disbelief. I think your mind is at least as sound as mine is. Wait, maybe that's a bad comparison.

"Some people will only get as organized as they need to," said Jimmy Rasmussen, Bank President. Everyone who wants to **can** become more organized, but not everyone can or even **should**, become a model of efficiency. For some, the strain of getting organized, of fitting into a mold, is too stressful. Fortunately, few of us are in that category, but for those who are, you probably haven't heard that before. Becoming clutterless is about becoming our authentic selves and taking responsibility for our lives. Most of us want to be more organized and are willing to take the necessary steps to do it. Even those of us who *want* to be become more organized **won't** do it, if we are in the wrong jobs for our talents and express our frustration in disorganization.

One of the basic facts about disorganization for clutterers is that it is not just about the piles on our desks. We've indulged in negative self-talk, ignored the emotions behind our actions, doubted our memories, and generally lived in fear of something we can't name.

Learn How You Learn

Often, we've been using the wrong learning techniques for our personalities. We're visual, auditory or kinesthetic people stuck in a logical world. Some of us don't even **like** certain letters of the alphabet! So why are we banging our heads against a wall trying to file in a way that is loaded with negative feelings?

I Don't Like to Take Tests!

Most clutterers don't. When we stumble across a test in a self-improvement or management book, we either dog-ear the page so we can come back to it "later" (meaning never), or in a rare moment of decisiveness, skip it. Aw heck, you can skip this one too (what am I gonna do, beat you with a stick?). If you really know what kind of learner you are, you don't need to take it.

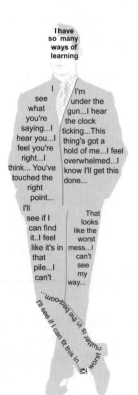

I have so many ways of learning

I see what you're saying...I hear you...I feel you're right...I think... You've touched the right point... I'll see if I can find it..I feel like it's in that pile...I can't

I'm under the gun...I hear the clock ticking...This thing's got a hold of me...I feel overwhelmed...I know I'll get this done...

That looks like the worst mess...I can't see my way...

...I'll see if I can fit this in....My clutter is in the bedroom...

Most of us don't really know, though. I'm convinced I'm a visual/logical learner. Girlfriends have often reminded me that I don't remember what color hair their has been (I swear it **was** red once), or ever notice what they have worn. I thought that was just being male. Don't even get them started on the "logical" spreadsheet calculations I made to decide which car to buy. ("If you take the square root of the gas mileage and multiply that by the mean average of cubic feet of trunk space ....")

These questions are short and simple. Many of us want to "do well" on tests and anticipate the "correct" answers. But Mr. Author, you said to anticipate in the first chapter! Belay that for the test. We figure out the pattern and try to make sure we fall into that pattern. Please don't do that. The first thing that comes to you is correct. There are no trick questions here:

1. When I agree with someone, I might say:
   - A. I see what you are saying.
   - B. I hear you.
   - C. I feel that you are right.
   - D. I think you are right.
   - E. I think you've touched on the right point.

2. When I feel under pressure, I might say:
   - A. I'm under the gun.
   - B. I hear the clock ticking.
   - C. I feel overwhelmed.
   - D. I know I will get this done.
   - E. This thing's got a hold of me.

3. When I look for something, I might say:
   - A. I'll see if I can find it.
   - B. That sounds familiar.
   - C. I feel as though it's in that pile.
   - D. I just know it's around here somewhere.
   - E. I know I can put my hands on it.

4. When I decide to try to clean up my office, I might think:
   - A. I can't clearly see my way.
   - B. That pile of clutter is calling to me.
   - C. I can't breathe. I'm drowning in clutter.
   - D. I can't believe I let it get this bad.
   - E. I'm going to get a handle on this mess.

5. When I try to declutter, I might think:
   - A. I'll start with the area that looks the worst.
   - B. I'm going to try a new technique I heard about.
   - C. This pile is calling to me.
   - D. I'll start at the left corner of my desk and work to the right.
   - E. I'll grab the first thing I see and start there.

6. At home, my worst clutter is:
    A. In my entrance.
    B. In my living room.
    C. In my bedroom.
    D. In my reading area.
    E. In my kitchen or garage.

7. When faced with a new demand on my time, I might think:
    A. I'll see if I can fit this in.
    B. It sounds like a lot of work to me.
    C. This doesn't seem fair.
    D. I have enough responsibilities. I don't know how this will fit in.
    E. I'll try to juggle some other things so I can squeeze it in.

8. When I meet someone for the first time, the initial thing that strikes me is:
    A. Their overall appearance.
    B. The sound of their voice.
    C. How sincere they seem to be.
    D. A combination of body language and what they are saying.
    E. The strength of their handshake.

9. When I shop for a new car, I am most attracted to:
    A. How it looks.
    B. The opinions of others I've talked to.
    C. An overall impression of how I'd feel about owning it.
    D. Gas mileage, reliability, and a good deal on financing.
    E. How it handles, how I feel behind the wheel.

10. I feel that I learn best through:
    A. Workshops, group presentations.
    B. Tapes to play in my car or at home.
    C. One-on-one discussions.
    D. Reading.
    E. Just doing it. Hands-on.

Results

You've probably already figured out that there are four broad categories of learning types. This is the basis of NLP (Neuro Linquistic Programing), as put forth by Tony Robbins and others.

 The key to learning and remembering is to find the way your brain works and utilize your dominant styles. No one is a pure type of course, but you will have a general tendency towards one style, with another coming in second. Use the following methods to help you to remember, to file, and to avoid cluttering. A main reason for disorganization is that we don't trust our memories. By learning our dominant learning style, we can improve our memories.

Number 10 fits all styles. Reading is auditory, visual, logical, and kinesthetic to some degree. If you choose "reading," but not many "D" answers, figure out your predominant learning sense from your other responses.

'A's—Visual

If you answered mainly 'A's, you are a visual learner. The question that gave you the most trouble was number 10, since visual people learn both from workshops and reading. So, even if you had a "D" for the last question, you are still visual.

'B's—Auditory

'B's are auditory learners. Because reading is an auditory skill for many of us (we mentally say the words as we read), in question 10, both B and D can be considered auditory answers. You learn best by verbal communication. You are more likely to get the most out of a conference, lecture, or tape. You probably have an extensive music collection. You wish this book was on tape.

'C's—Emotional

'C's are emotional learners. There are two types within this broad category. **Inter**personal types are concerned with how things affect others. **Intra**personal types internalize everything. How things affect them inside is the most important. This can be a good thing, if they have a highly intuitive, sixth sense, or if a self-defeating behavior if their self-esteem is so low that it goes up and down like a yo-yo with every decision.

'D's—Logical

'D's learn best by understanding "why" something works or needs to be done. They like to have a lot of graphs, flowcharts, and orderly steps to get something done. Few disorganized people are truly logical, but many of us have a mistaken belief that we are. I fit in this category. Most of us should count this as a secondary skill, since we are probably hoping we will be logical when we grow up. Maybe we will.

Logical people are organized and efficient. We often tell ourselves (me included) that what we are doing is logical. We take logical steps to arrive at an illogical conclusion. If you answered with a lot of 'D's, then check your number two responses. They are probably more accurate. You are probably an "A" but want to be a "D." If your talent is to be logical, you can develop that trait. But to get started, you'll have to learn to get organized to know what it feels like. Thus, you should apply the "A" techniques until they become habit and the "D" traits will start to emerge as your true self. In a sense, visual is more logical than the others. We feel that we can trust what we see more than what we hear or feel.

'E's—Kinesthetic

'E's are kinesthetic learners. They have to have some kind of physical contact to enhance learning. Great typists are kinesthetic. Graphic artists work in that mode combined with the visual mode. Kinesthetics would rather shop in a store than buy online. They want to see a working model before saying yes to a design.

But I thought I was something else

If your answers don't seem to be "right," you didn't flunk. Some of us don't really know how we learn and are more likely to have put down how we "think" we learn. Later, we'll do a visualization exercise that will clarify it for us. If there is a discrepancy between your answers here and the results of the visualization, go with the style that is dominant in your visualization. We are complicated people and this little test is only a first step on the journey to understanding ourselves.

Clutterer Traits and How We Can Turn Them Into Assets

A Different Sense of Time. Clutterers truly march to a different drummer. Time for us is more expansive. We have a hard time meeting finishing lines (deadlines in the old terminology) See Chapter 4.

Turn this into an asset: Change time from an enemy to a friendly face. Creating an expanded pie chart in a spreadsheet that looks like Pac Man eating Time makes it fun. (In the example, the task was the number of words I had to write for this book. Time was days to submission). As each day passed the Task "ate up" the Time. See Chapter 14 for more ways to de-fang time.

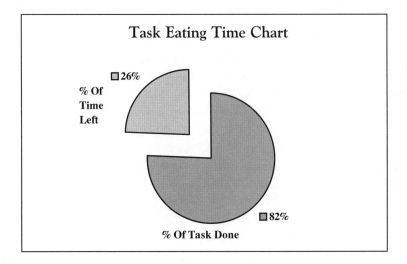

The mathematically observant will notice that the two figures don't add up to 100 percent, as in a traditional pie chart. They aren't supposed to. The Time Left changes just once a day. The amount of work done changes hourly. Time has become static. Our work is more important and is what we have control over. The more we work, the more we devour time.

Selective memories: We commonly say that we have terrible memories. This isn't completely accurate. We remember things by the **emotional value** we place on them. In the office setting, we are more likely to remember the Johnson project because of how we feel about Johnson or the people associated with it. If a project or file has no emotions attached to it, we are more likely to forget it. At home, we cannot let go of things because we remember who gave them to us, or the times we had in a certain dress, jacket, and so on. The thing **becomes** the emotion.

Turn this into an asset: Assign a positive emotion or picture (the visual component) to every project, every file you want to remember. If you think something your boss gave you to do is silly, visualize it as a game of hopscotch or something childish. If you have a project that is dead serious, think of it in a spiritual sense of Heaven or the Great Beyond. If you have to go on a business trip, imagine it as flying like Peter Pan, or unlimited freedom. If you chose the later, you haven't been on enough business trips, but enjoy your illusions while you can.

Internal chatter: Our minds are seldom quiet, unless we are completely focused (like when writing, designing a big project, debugging a computer program). Most things are not that important. Our minds work fast and most projects are just too slow for us.

Turn this into an asset: Pay attention to the chatter for a few minutes and see how silly it is. A typical scenario might be: we imagine a project not getting done, see ourselves losing our jobs, asking our brother-in-law for a loan. Laugh at it, then get back to work with a cleared head. Sometimes, turning up the outside noise (like playing music, opening a window) can stop the chatter, especially for some people with AD/HD.

Easily bored: If something doesn't keep our attention, we can't stay focused on it. We don't want to finish it. Routine tasks like filing, clearing out old files, organizing our activities on a day-to-day basis (the traditional to-do list) are lower than low on our priority list. We feel like Secretariat being asked to pull a plough.

Turn this into an asset: Make the routine chores into games. Assign yourself five points for clearing out five files. When you've accumulated 100 points, reward yourself. (No, you can't make each file worth 25 points). Reward yourself for working on something you don't like for 30 minutes by taking a 10-minute break. Take a walk outside or down the hall with a file folder in one hand and a pen in another. That at least looks like you are doing something work-like.

Creative: We have vivid imaginations. We just don't channel them very well. We spend a lot of time daydreaming, **thinking** about projects, but not doing the actual work that could make them reality. The action part is not as interesting as the creating part. Details bore us.

Turn this into an asset: Use that imagination! Thinking is a part of business that isn't limited to the CEOs and assorted muckety-mucks. Write down your thoughts and see if they don't present a better way to do things.

Degrees of Cluttering or Disorganization

The degree of our disorganization will determine how much effort we need to put into changing our behavior.

Mildly disorganized. If you are fortunate enough to be one of these people, then a little tweaking like using your dominant learning skill, improving decision-making, or visualization, is all you need. You are the kind of person who generally maintains a neat desk (with a few scattered papers to add flavor), knows where 90 percent of your files are, and would rather not have a messy desk.

You probably only need to spend about five percent of your time on organizing to improve your work life. Your home is probably not in need of any work at all.

A situational clutterer. You can keep pretty good track of where things are, but when faced with deadlines or extra pressure, you react by losing papers and feeling overwhelmed. Cheer up! The problem isn't that you are chronically disorganized. It is that you have chosen this method to react to doing something you don't want to do, or are afraid of failing at. We can fix this by changing the way you relate to tasks and lowering your misplaced perfectionism.

About 20 percent of disorganized people were neat until a traumatic event changed their lives. They became messy after the death of a loved one, loss of a job or relationship, or a divorce. While this is thorny emotional ground, it's easier to change the cluttering behavior because we know the obvious psychological roots. Yours aren't buried deep in your psychic garden. With a little psychological digging, you can release your uncluttered self and return to your previously uncluttered life. A word of caution—don't start until you are ready. Your cluttering may be protecting you from dealing with emotions you can't deal with right now. Once you get started, it won't take you much time at all to get back to normal.

Home- or office- only clutterer. You seem to live two lives. You're relatively neat at home and cluttered at the office, or vice-versa. This shows that you have the ability to get and stay organized, but there is a deeper psychological reason why you clutter in one area or the other.

You'll probably have to initially devote 20 percent of your time to understanding what's going on and why it is expressed in disorganization. You've got some ingrained habits that can be changed when you know what's behind them. Once you're back on track, staying there will only require periodic checks.

Every aspect of your life overwhelms you. Congratulations! You are a real clutterer. You spend more time **looking** for things than **doing** things. Your office and home are cluttered. You will get better, but it will require some real work on your part. You'll have to understand why you clutter and decide you want to change the behavior. If you really want to change, you can. Don't change because your boss is on your back. Change because you want a better life.

The reasons you're disorganized are deep-seated and have to be faced before you can make any permanent progress. Don't worry, I'm not suggesting Freudian analysis. I won't ask you to relate your clutter to your relationship with your mother. While we are on the subject of mothers, no, cluttering is not genetic. It may be learned behavior, but even that doesn't hold up statistically. About half of clutterers came from cluttering families (or obsessively neat families—the flip side of the same coin).

You can make positive changes **immediately** and work on the rest over time. The practical visualization and memory tools here will help you today. Behavioral modification will take some time. Cluttering is a habit. Not cluttering is also a habit. It's hard to change alone. Consider a self-help group like Clutterless (*www.clutterless.org*) and/or psychological counseling. **Changing your outside without changing your inside is only temporary.** Disorganization has stolen your life. You may have to spend 30 percent of your time fighting what comes naturally to you—cluttering. Oh my gosh, you may say. That's a lot of time. That 30 percent investment will result in a 200 percent improvement in the way you work and feel about yourself. Do you get that good a return from your mutual fund?

An uncontrollable clutterer. Some of us will never get organized. The stress of trying to fit into someone else's mold is just too much. Before you jump up and shout "Hooray! I can stop trying!" and upset your cluttered desk, think about this for a minute. If you honestly try and don't really want to change, accept it. Accept the consequences as well. You will always under-earn. You will never know the joy of living to even half your potential. But maybe that's not important to you. Maybe you have made such a relationship with your demons that you don't need any other kind. Who's to judge?

So What's the Secret?

Most of us have seriously tried to get organized and not succeeded for any length of time. You could have already lost jobs because of your cluttering. So you bought this book just in case "the secret" was in it. I am sorry. The secret is not here—it is within you. You already know the secret. You've got to want to.

A Simpler Life?

Sometimes the best answer may be to find a job that is essentially without deadlines (nearly impossible), or one where you can work on your own schedule as a freelance worker. A growing number of people are "temps" on a full-time basis. Some temporary agencies even have health care now. The advantage is that your jobs are varied and if you don't fit into the corporate structure, you can move on.

Some people have decided that working to own too many "things" is occupying too much of their lives. They've become part of the "Voluntary Simplicity Movement" (*www.simpleliving.net*). Living the simple life puts more value on **how** you live than what you own. Is your BMW *clutter*? It could be if what you have to do to get it and maintain it is interfering with your Really Big Goals. Everything you own requires time for purchasing or maintaining. Maybe you have allowed your stuff own you instead of you owning your stuff. If that's the case, then downsizing might be the solution for you.

Negative Payoffs

Most of us won't admit that we stay disorganized because we want to, but there is always a reason why we do what we do. Sometimes, we clutter because we get what we want by doing it. "What?" You shout, "I don't get any joy out of being this way!" Before you throw this book across the room, hear me out. I've been where you are, and so have many others who have overcome this challenge.

Learning to be organized is like painting your house. You could just slap some paint (the "10 quick-fix steps to being organized" approach) on it. In a few months it looks as bad as before and you have to redo the process. Doing it right takes digging under the surface. You look for dry rot, reattach loose boards, and sandblast the old paint away. By the time you're ready to paint, it looks worse than when you started. You've torn off the surface, exposing the bare bones. You may discover that the roof needs to be replaced, which isn't what you started out to do. But the leaky roof is part of the house as a whole, so you might as well fix it while you're at it.

So it is with dealing with your cluttering. You may have to strip off the protective coating of excuses and rationalizations that have kept you from getting to the interior.

Think About These Things

▶ **You get attention from others in the victim role.**

Co-workers make jokes about your messy desk. You get a nickname like "Messy Melissa." Your boss spends more of his time with you than with a non-cluttering employee. When faced with a deadline, you count on another employee rescuing you.

▶ **You avoid extra work, or being given assignments with a high visibility.**

Your boss knows that you are easily overwhelmed, so doesn't pile too much on you. Since you'd rather avoid the spotlight, you don't have to worry about doing a project that means a great deal to your company. Thus, you are able to plod along in relative obscurity, which suits you just fine.

▶ **You always have an excuse for being late, or half-finishing projects.**

"I could have finished it, but was missing the _____ file." "I just need another day or two to finish. Can I get an extension?"

▶ **You are an adrenaline junkie.**

"I work best under pressure. Sure I procrastinate, but I always get the job done on time. I may put in sixteen-hour days, but I've never missed a deadline."

Drs. Hemfelt, Minirth, and Meier call this an applauded behavior, "a crisis high." (*We Are Driven.* Thomas Nelson Publishers, 1991.) By waiting until the last minute, you charge an otherwise mundane task with drama. Since you always come through, you are rewarded with pats on the back, promotions, and raises.

Deadline is the operative word here. You are literally shortening your life. We weren't meant to live on adrenaline rushes. Our bodies can only take it for so long. We've got to channel this energy into ways that make our lives more fulfilling.

Okay, Let's Get Started

Now that you've got some background on the *why* of your own personal disorganization, we can begin to work on the *how* of changing it. Onward!

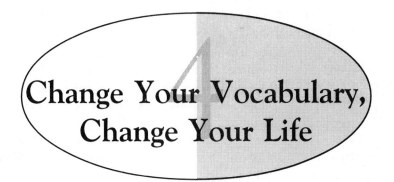

Change Your Vocabulary, Change Your Life

*Working hard and getting no result is very punishing
to the mind. In the movie,* The Last Castle, *Robert Redford
is made to move thousands of pounds of rocks from
one side of a path to the other, and back again.
Clutterers are like that. They are only rotating the clutter.*

—Kent, a clutterer's husband.

Key Concepts

1. Doing is more likely to get done than "To-Do"-ing.

2. Deadlines are for the dying.

3. Personal and work are intertwined.

4. You can make decisions.

Doing Is Better Than To-Do

Jimmy Rasmussen is very organized and typical of the type of person for whom a "To-Do" list is an indispensable tool. "I get frustrated and feel unproductive when I am not organized. The To-Do List is critical. I always have a To-Do list and try to return all calls ASAP, even if it's only one call." He never loses sight of what is really important—customers. He's flexible enough to override an arbitrary list of what he thinks needs to be done in the beginning of the day by adapting to what happens during the day.

The most important thing on our "Doing" or "To-Do" list is to take care of those things that will validate the way we do business. **Business, like cluttering, isn't about things; it's about people.**

A Doing List as long as a letter to Santa Claus

"To-Do" lists work great—for some people. Organized people rely heavily on them. For some disorganized people, a To-Do list is the only tool they know. Putting a To-Do list in the hands of the chronically disorganized is like giving a computer to a Neanderthal. We dutifully make them, secretly believing that whatever we put on the list will magically get done by the end of the day. For us, they are more like letters to Santa.

Aside from the fact that a clutterer loses his "To-Do" list in his clutter, the name implies "ought to." Our natural rebelliousness flares up. "Nobody's gonna tell me what I ought to do." In Texas, when we say we're "fixing to do" something, it means we've advanced beyond thinking about it, but aren't ready to take action. It's an intermediate step, something that should appeal to clutterers. "Fixing to do" something keeps us from committing to getting it done. Some people feel the same way about "To-Do" lists.

Replace your "To-Do" list with a "Doing" list. We are actively doing those things that need to be done. This little bit of semantics can change our attitude. Sure, it's just a couple of words, but words are what make us. We engage in self-talk all the time. Psychiatrists tell us that by changing our negative self-talk to positive self-talk, we can make a first step to changing negative behaviors (we still have to take action, but that comes later). They suggest changing "I can't" phrases to "I can" phrases. A "Doing" list is a set of actions we are taking, right now. And right now is the only time we really have.

Keep your Doing List Simple

"If you spend hours writing down all the things that need to be done, you have only wasted time painting an overwhelming picture that makes you want to do anything but confront it. You feel "stuck," and that is a very hopeless feeling. The more you neglect that list, the angrier you get at yourself. The result? Depression, anxiety, substance

abuse...etc. The answer? Make a list of what you can real-
istically do the following day, do it, and feel proud of your
accomplishment!"
—Anonymous e-mail

I've put six and seven items on the sample Doing lists. Studies have
shown that most people can remember five to nine items and seven is average. The idea of a Doing list is to make what you want to do concrete. If
you have to keep referring back to your list, it is too long. I made it even
easier for us by filling in two of the blanks. See, you should only put four or
five things on it. Even that may be too much. Tom Sullivan suggests, "Make
a list of ten things you want to do today. Then cross out seven. If you get
three important things done, you'll have accomplished a lot."

Words Without Actions Won't Cut It

Just changing the words won't make any list work for us if we don't
use them properly. We've all seen the people who carry 10-pound Day-
Timers with "To-Do" lists that would challenge a team of mules. The more
technologically advanced have replaced the paper Day-Timers with (Personal Digital Assistants (PDAs). They weigh less, but carry more stuff to
do. Instead of ten-pounds, they cart megabytes of things they "have" to do.

Stephen Covey, in *The 7 Habits Of Highly Effective People* said there
our lives are in quadrants. Quadrant one is urgent and important, two is
not urgent but important, three is urgent, but not important, and four is
neither urgent nor important. He's a brilliant writer and his matrix is very
good. I'm proposing a hybrid of that and a "To-Do" list. It should work
for disorganized people better because it requires fewer decisions. By
putting both long-term and short-term goals together, we can see how
they mesh together. We're going to break our business and personal life
goals apart and when we have clarity about them, put them back together
again. Then our job will be to make them work together.

On a legal pad, in your PDA, your contact manager or word proces-
sor, make a list of the things you want to accomplish in your business life.
(See the example on page 56.) Five things you know about are plenty. The
third, "declutter one area," and the seventh, "the unexpected," are absolutely necessary. They are in the order of priorities for a reason. If we put
"decluttering" at the bottom, we may never get to it. Yet, that is the major
issue here.

My Daily Doing List		
Doing Have to	Learning Ought to	Planning Want to
1.		
2.		
3. Declutter one area.	Analyze my cluttering.	Organize my work life to emphasize those areas where I am already neat.
4.		
5.		
6.		
7. The unexpected.		

Plan on the Unexpected

"The unexpected" is at the bottom, but it won't stay there. As in Mr. Rasmussen's example, something could happen that moves it to a higher priority. Far too often we start our day with a definite list of priorities and things we want to get done. We are making great headway, feeling proud of ourselves. Then, at 11:45, we get a call from our West Coast division informing us that the shipment they needed to start production has been held up in customs. A flight is canceled and our key sales person can't make an important presentation. We start feeling sick and have to go home. By having "the unexpected" written into our Doing list, we don't have to feel like we are breaking our stride by taking care of it.

Less Is More

Putting more items on the list makes it overwhelming. If you get five immediate things done at work in one day, you've done a good job. You'll probably do three. If we spend all our time doing the "Have to," we'll never get to the other two columns. The time a project takes to complete will expand to the amount of time we have to complete it. So, let's spend a little time in the other two columns.

Instead of racing to get the "Have to" done in order, do two or three of them, switch to the "Ought to," and do one of those. Then switch back.

If you're feeling stymied at some point because what you need to do depends on someone else's actions, take a break and concentrate on a "Want to" for awhile. If we never get to the "Want to," they will never get done.

There are blank spaces, because we will probably learn something from doing tasks that lead to learning or planning. Eventually, we may have only one "Have to," since we've done such a good job on the longer term.

My Daily Doing List		
Doing **Have to**	Learning **Ought to**	Planning **Want to**
1. Get started on the Quimby report.	What can I do to make report writing less drudgery—for myself and my employees?	Expand my business or career.
2. Call or e-mail my salespeople.	Learn a better way to reward and motivate sales people.	Determine what our sales' weaknesses and strengths are, in order to expand or condense our sales force.
3. Declutter one area of my workspace: desk, mail, in-box drawer, etc.	Get out of my office and see what visible clutter exists among my employees. Analyze that.	Explore the company's, my own, and my managers' priorities. Are they clear? Do they contribute to mental clutter?
4. Return calls.	Focus on callers.	Find out why I get so many calls. Is something unclear in our materials? Are my goals not clear to all our people?
5. Talk to the accountant about our 401(k) Plan.		Find the best way to reward employees.
6. Attend a meeting at 3:30.	Focus on meeting.	Learn how or teach our managers how to run fewer, more productive meetings.
7. The unexpected.		If the unexpected is frequently a major issue, analyze why that is. See #3

An Executive or Manager's Doing List

Tasks segue from the immediate to the long-term. When we write a "Doing" goal, there is probably something that we need to learn from, or about, that activity. We could probably do some long-term planning that would cut down on the number of "Doing" items.

My Daily Doing List		
Doing Have to	Learning Ought to	Planning Want to
1. Get details on the Quimby account to my boss.	Learn a more efficient way to prepare these reports so I can spend less time on them.	Expand my career, so I'll be receiving details on accounts from my subordinates.
2. Call or e-mail customers.	Learn to listen and resond to customers better.	Initiate a report with what I've learned to show management how we could do a better job for our customers. This will move the goal above forward.
3. Declutter one area that is in my control.	Is the clutter caused by me, others, or the company policies?	What can I do to keep this clutter from happening in the first place?
4. Sort mail, faxes, and memos that need to go to my boss. File those items that have been acted upon.	Check if my filing system still makes sense.	Research a more streamlined way to cut down on the first group. Present my ideas to management. (See #1.)
5. Generate letters, spreadsheets, or other computer-related tasks.		Research ways to work with computers more efficiently. Expand my computer skills. (See #1.)
6. Attend a meeting at 3:30.	Listen.	I am afraid to speak up in meetings. Research ways to improve my speaking skills: classes, Toastmasters, etc. (See #1.)
7. The unexpected.		

A Front-line Employee's Doing List

For those of us in non-management positions, everything we do is related to those above us. For many of us, the long-term goal is to move up in the workplace. By doing the expected (Have to), and the more than expected (Ought to), we can further our long-term goals (Want to).

But Wait! There's More!

The techniques above will take care of our 9-5 lives. If we want to live balanced lives, we have to have a decision-making matrix. We often hear about making time for family, but those of us who are single feel neglected. We are just as important as those with a life-partner and kids. For us, having a social life is just as important as a family life is to them.

My Daily Doing List		
Doing **Have to**	Learning **Ought to**	Planning **Want to**
1. Spend time with family, friends, or dating.	Be able to have a social or family life.	Find ways to have more time for those I care about.
2. Spend time on myself, my growth, my spiritual life.		Decide what my perfect personal and spiritual life is.
3. Declutter one area of the house, garage, yard.	Is there an area of the house that reflects my dissatisfaction with my job, personal life?	If my cluttering reflects the rest of my life, what is the conflict? How can I change it?
4. Sort mail. Pay bills. File. Pick up, do laundry, clean.	Organize my computer.	Research a more streamlined way to cut down on the group in the first column. (See #1.)
5. Write personal letters, e-mails or other computer tasks.		Research ways to work with comuters more efficiently. Expand my computer skills. (See #1.)
6. Do my volunteer work. Help others in some way.		Determine how much time I really have and allocate it correctly. (See #1.)
7. The unexpected.		

Personal Life Doing List

Right now, it is important to see the Big Picture. We are often more clear about our daily goals at work than we are at home. Once we've visualized the Big Picture clearly in our heads, we can make a daily plan for home. Business has specific goals (customer service, make a profit for the stockholders, public service, etc.). We get bogged down in the minutia in our home lives. Let's approach it from another angle.

It's Decision Time!

Now that we've gotten some clarity on what we have to do and what we want to do, we can start to make some decisions. Chances are, we've

been rolling along, letting life happen to us, instead of taking charge of our lives. We hate to make decisions. We're afraid that when we commit to something that we'll be wrong and pay some sort of dire consequences. As psychiatrists tell us, we are vague about exactly **what** the consequences will be. What we don't take into account is that we are already paying far more serious consequences by inaction. We exhibit disorganized behaviors that sabotage our efforts to live fulfilled lives, professionally and personally. Before we can begin to make decisions, we need to take an inventory and decide what we want to decide.

Our daily decisions are not part of some psychic permanent record. Santa Claus or God is not keeping score, tallying whether we've been wrong or right. People change their minds all the time. Before we can change our minds, we have to make them up. No decision is irrevocable. No decision is perfect. We act as if our world would collapse if we took a stand and made a mistake. It won't and we will. Chances are, we will make far more right decisions than wrong ones. We already have. But, in our beautiful, negative, self-limiting ways, we have chosen to remember the wrong ones.

Are We Conflicted?

Compare your business Doing list with your personal Doing list. Do they conflict? If so, decide which is really important to you. You cannot be effective at either if you are conflicted. The conflicts are usually in goals one and two. You may not be able to reconcile them immediately. It will take some serious thinking about what is really important to you. Take all the time you need, but don't keep trying to live a conflicted life. Conflicts come out in unexpected ways and most certainly contribute to our cluttering.

CONFLICTS BETWEEN MY PERSONAL LIFE AND BUSINESS LIFE		
CONFLICTS/INSIGHTS	BELIEFS	SOLUTIONS
1. I want to spend time with family, friends, or dating.	If I work more to do a great job and make more money, I'll buy time.	Can I delegate more work to a trusted subordinate or eliminate secondary tasks to free more time?
2. I want more time to spend on myself, my growth, my spiritual life.	See #1.	See #1. Can I arrange flex-hours so I can take classes, have time for Yoga, exercise, or meditation?
3. I don't see any resolution between business and personal goals. They conflict too much.	I have to have a job that provides security for my family and my retirement.	Look for a job that provides for my needs, but doesn't take all my time. I could redefine my current position and present it to management proving they would benefit.
4. Such a job doesn't exist for me.	I need self-employment that will provide the above.	I can evaluate my skills and needs to determine self-employment opportunities.
5. My overhead is just too high.	Self-employment is unlikely to meet my expenses.	Maybe simplifying my life and lowering my needs is part of the solution.

If You Hit the Mark 40 percent of the Time, You're in the Big Leagues

Athletes get paid millions of dollars for only hitting the mark less than half the time. A baseball player who makes more hits than outs doesn't exist. A basketball great who sinks a basket every time he gets the ball doesn't exist. A golfer who shoots 18 more often than he takes 70 strokes to finish the game would be a god.

So, step up to the plate and do something. Otherwise you will never make it to the big leagues. To participate in your life in a big league way, you may have to change your stance or adjust your grip, but you can do it— if you really want to. There are two types of people who read self-help books. One reads all the self-improvement books printed (and we authors thank you), but only applies the principles in them for a short time. Other readers take the ideas that work for them disregard the rest, and move forward.

Deadlines Are for Cemeteries

Once, I was the landscaper for a cemetery in New Orleans. I wanted to plant some posies in the middle of it. Big John, the good old boy who ran the operation said, "Bubba, you can't do that. Them purty little flowers will grow over the dead line. We'll just have to dig 'em up." The "dead line" was the delineation of where the landscaping (preplanning) ended and the graves (the object of the business) started.

Change "deadlines" to **"finish lines."** Why attach a negative concept to the very things we want to get done? Everyone loves to cross the finish line. When I ran marathons, I wouldn't have been so enthused about punishing my body, if I was reaching for a deadline. The more we make work into a game, the more we enjoy it. The more we enjoy it, the less likely we are to clutter it up.

Be You

We've all been exhorted to "Be the Best." "Being the Best" implies comparison. Comparison turns into competition. Clutterers are generally not competitive. We've got enough competition going on inside ourselves. When our self-image is fragile, competition can be harmful. I have to fight my competitive persona. It stems from my insecurities.

When I find myself comparing myself to other authors or speakers, it turns into a better/worse competition. "I'm better than they are," makes me feel good. "Gee, I wish I was as smart as they are," makes me feel insecure. When I accept that I am unique and the best me there is, I can learn. And learning is what life is all about. When I read the same authors or really listen to the same speakers, expecting to learn something from their unique presentations, I gain.

Affirm yourself: "I am the perfect (say your name)." Say it again using your own nicknames. Be playful by saying your full legal name, your birth name, all the names you've heard yourself called (except those requiring an expletive). How does each one feel? Walk around, spend the day in that persona.

I want you to be you. You are the only you there is. By definition, you are the best you there is. If you are true to yourself; if you live according to your authentic self, you will be the best you can be. You don't need to compare yourself to anyone. This isn't an excuse for not being best. It is a faster way to get there. We aren't in competition with others because we are all part of the human drama, playing our part. Play your part. Do your part. That is the best anyone can do.

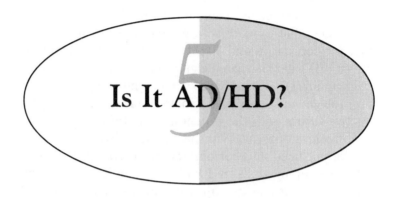

Is It AD/HD?

*ADD manifests as an exaggeration
of tendencies we all have.*

—A medical professional with AD/HD

As I said in the Chapter One, it is statistically unlikely that you have AD/HD. As I also said, only medical testing and diagnosis will tell you if you have it. But, since this question comes up at every workshop, every Clutterless meeting, and about a quarter of my e-mail, it deserves elaboration. Of all the clutterers I personally know, only five have been diagnosed with AD/HD. They are all professionals, holding down good jobs. They are all perfect examples of how AD/HD or cluttering are not excuses for not being the authentic you—the best you. They have learned to use their unique traits in positive ways, in jobs that don't force them to be someone they are not.

AD/HD and Cluttering

"Being on my own enables me to clutter to my fullest potential. I had an "administrative assistant" for almost an entire year. She was the best friend I could have dreamed of. She helped encourage progress in our office. I lost her services about year ago. My skills have slipped back to only about 20 percent of what they were with her support. At home, my behavior is beginning to "enable" my 8 year-old

son's to clutter. He was diagnosed with AD/HD in 1998.
Meanwhile, I've been treated for depression and anxiety. I
have been able to work with my therapist to understand
that my depression and anxiety may be co-dependent on
my AD/HD and associated clutter. It has reached a serious
point in my 11-year marriage where I must get control of
my problem and deal with it's roots, or face a lonely, unproductive future with the potential to harm my son's own
healthy development. With his already obvious AD/HD,
he doesn't need another obstacle in the development of
effective coping skills. If I had been able to address my
AD/HD as early as he can, I do not think that I would
have as much difficulty as I face now."
—Toni, Office Manager with AD/HD

What Is ADD?

Clutterers and those with AD/HD have different ways of looking at
things than most people, which contributes to their disorganization at
work. While one goal of this book is to help us to improve our skills and
use our unique talents, a larger one is to help us recognize when we need
to move on. No matter how much better our organizational skills get,
unless we are being true to our authentic selves, we will be frustrated.

Wilma Fellman, M.Ed., LPC, is a Career and Life-Planning Counselor
specializing in working with ADD or AD/HD adults in Troy, Michigan,
(*www.findingacareer.com*), and author of *The Other Me: Poetic Thoughts on
ADD for Adults, Kids and Parents,* and *Finding A Career That Works For
You.* She is on the Executive Board of the Michigan Career Development
Association. Feldman agrees that some of the symptoms of cluttering and
those of AD/HD adults have similarities. She thinks it is important to emphasize our strengths and work on our weaknesses.

"We have the choice to live our lives 'leading with our strengths,'
or offering our challenges as excuses for our failures. We can refer
to ourselves as 'disabled' or we can show the world our special 'gifts.'
As a career counselor, I work to assist clients in identifying their
special talents. If we, as humans, are made of hundreds of 'puzzle
pieces,' does it not make sense to first define ourselves by referring
to those parts that shine brightly? When we look at Christopher

Reeve, who was paralyzed when he was thrown off a horse, do we see disability, or do we see outstanding strength of will and character that catapults him into productive action?"

I've mentioned that maybe we are just in the wrong jobs, either because they conflict with our life goals and our true selves, or because they require a degree of organization or highly structured style of working that is just too stressful for clutterers.

AD/HD symptoms will sound very familiar to chronic clutterers, and indeed, to everyone who experiences too much stress. But before we get into the "symptoms," let's take a look at the whole person who may have AD/HD. Like the table in Chapter 2, what can be a less than ideal trait may have a very positive aspect, if used appropriately.

The ADD "Personality"

Two very good books on ADD are: *You Mean I'm Not Lazy, Stupid or Crazy?!* by Kate Kelly and Peggy Ramundo (Simon & Schuster, New York, 1993) and *ADD in the Workplace.* AD/HD is a manifestation of tendencies we all have.

Both books warn of self-diagnosis. When tests for AD/HD were given in schools, it seemed like every student was an AD/HD candidate. Kelly and Ramundo warn of a rush to self-diagnosis thusly: "Anyone can sometimes have lapse in memory, act impulsively, or have difficulty concentrating. The problem with AD/HD is one of degree and persistence of the symptoms over time and across varying situations."

There are many types of personalities who have AD/HD to some degree or another. AD/HD can be controlled with medication. Some of the overlapping symptoms can also be manifested in depression, anxiety, and times when we have a little too much stress.

So, What's It Like to Have AD/HD?

In his article, *What's It Like To Have ADD? (www.add.org/content/abc/hallowell.htm)*, Edward M. Hallowell, M.D., provided the very best description of what it is like to have AD/HD: "Often these people are highly imaginative and intuitive. They have a 'feel' for things, a way of seeing right into the heart of matters while others have to reason their way along methodically. This is the man or woman who makes million dollar deals in a catnap and pulls them off the next day."

Could It Just Be Trying to Multi-task?

According to the online business news magazine, *The Industry Standard (www.thestandard.com)*, "The multitasking nature of work in the new economy may be causing workers to experience symptoms resembling those of Attention Deficit Disorder."

An article on *www.cnn.com* said that, "But newly released results of scientific studies in multitasking indicate that carrying on several duties at once may, in fact, reduce productivity, not increase it."

Some AD/HD Traits and Solutions That Also Apply to Clutterers

This is not a complete collection of "symptoms" or clinical solutions. It's a start. It is what I have learned through observation, interviews, and reading about our similar ways of viewing the world with some practical suggestions on how to deal with them. Most of these practical solutions are elaborated upon throughout this book. This "quick look" will help people with AD/HD appreciate that we are all in this together. There are solutions. We just have to work at them. If you have been diagnosed with AD/HD, your therapist will guide you through more detailed ways to work on these issues.

▶ **Poor awareness of "clock time."**

Clutterers and people with AD/HD run late, miss deadlines, and generally do not work by the same clock as the rest of the world. This can be due to the "one last thing to do" that takes longer than we expect, underestimating the time a project will take, or hyperfocusing and losing track of time. The techniques of "about" time scheduling in Chapter 13 help you learn how to free yourself from the bondage of time and still be polite and "on time."

▶ **Internal chatter.**

Clutterers seem to have this to a lesser degree than people with AD/HD. Quieting the mind can be achieved by meditation and writing. The process of writing slows the brain down and helps it to focus. Many AD/HD people work better when there is more noise around them. They can concentrate in crowded restaurants that would drive other people nuts. They can get work done if there is music playing. One solution (besides moving the office to a cafeteria) is to play music at work. Home-workers will have no difficulty in doing this, though we need to remember to turn it off when we get a phone call. In the corporate environment, headphones make sense. A noisy keyboard (suggested in the advice for auditory learners) is a good first step.

▶ **Hyperfocusing.**

Have you ever been so wrapped up in what you were doing that you tuned out the world around you? Then you have hyperfocused. This isn't a "bad" thing. It enables us to really concentrate and get some projects done. When I write, nothing exists for me outside my words and thoughts. All people could benefit from this tendency from time to time.

As a physician assistant clutterer who has been diagnosed with AD/HD put it, "This is a valuable trait in the operating room. When I've got a patient's artery in my hand, that has to be my whole world. I don't want to have to wonder where the clamps are, or be distracted about some reports that are due. When I walk out of the operating theatre, it's like I'm entering a different world. People think I am a ditz."

▶ **Difficulty in focusing on long-term tasks.**

People with AD/HD and clutterers are often insightful people who can imagine a brilliant course of action, but have a hard time staying focused to put it through. They are better at shorter tasks that result in more immediate results. If you absolutely have to complete a task that requires attention to details, break it up into smaller segments. We can concentrate better when we can see the goal. Take breaks.

▶ **Forgetting.**

Write things down. Use the memory techniques suggested in this book, tailored for your own personality. Have people repeat instructions to you verbally and write them down. Your memory is better than you think; you just haven't been using the right ways to access it.

▶ **Hyperactivity.**

This could also be described as having a high energy level. Gee, that's a positive trait. This is what most people think of when they imagine an AD/HD person. Restlessness. Constant movement. With medication, this is often lessened or disappears. The AD/HD people I know who take meidcation don't seem overwhelmingly restless. This is also something that non-AD/HD people do. Have you ever watched a presenter play with her pen, jiggle the change in his pocket? It's a common expression of discomfort, so don't read much into it.

▶ **Gotta move around.**

So? What's the harm in leaving your workstation and walking around? It's healthier from an ergonomic standpoint. Walking improves the circulation and blood flow to the brain, which helps us think. All people should learn from this "ADD characteristic." They are on the right track.

▶ **Talking without thinking.**

This one makes me wonder if many politicians don't have ADD. Sometimes the overwhelming need to communicate can result in saying things that are, well, less than tactful. It's hard to break, but you could try counting to 10 before blurting out "Boy, that's a stupid idea." Chances are, you will get distracted before you get to 10, or the conversation will have moved on. Talking nonstop is another manifestation of this tendency. So is being super-quiet. See, I told you it was complicated. To correct this will take a lot of effort, but one way is to use your intuition to guide you. If you listen to your inner voice before using your outer voice, you might find fewer faux pas happening.

▶ **Easily distracted.**

Clutterers often start a project, jump to another and then to another. So it is with ADD folks. We end up with many unfinished projects cluttering our landscape, physically and mentally. Too often, the projects are longer-term than we suspected, so we lose interest. The idea of breaking them down into bite-sized bits can help.

No Matter What the Challenges, There Are Solutions

People with ADD and chronic cluttering are all around us. We are greater in numbers than even we think. Some of us have learned to deal with our differences so effectively that others don't even suspect. We can be successful in any field that really speaks to us. We can overcome our so-called limitations and utilize our assets so that we can be valuable members of society. Or, we can use our differences as excuses for remaining unemployed, under-employed, unhappy, frustrated, and so on. The choice is ours. Ideally, this book will show you how to make those choices.

What Works?
What Doesn't?

Q: *What hasn't worked for you?*

A: *Anything that uses words like "Have to," "Should," "Ought to," "Need to," "Why don't you," "You should have," "What are you doing," "Any observation that starts out with YOU," stops me from listening. It puts me on the defensive and makes me want to protect and defend the way I do things.*

—Response to online survey question

Key Concepts

1. You are more organized than you think.

2. Home and office are related.

3. You've been taught myths about organizing.

4. A system will only work if it is *your* system.

No one is completely disorganized. We all have some (shudder) **organized** traits. I haven't met one clutterer who wasn't neat in some area of her life. But we like to label ourselves "disorganized" or "messy," so we ignore our strengths and concentrate on our weaknesses.

Everyone gets disorganized sometimes

Even organized people are sometimes overwhelmed. Kim Haas, Womans-Net CEO, (*http://Womans-Net.com*) said, "Since I multitask, it's easy for clutter to build up, but as I complete one project and move to the next, the clutter begins to disappear. When my desk is very cluttered because of various tasks all running at the same time, I begin to feel over-whelmed. I will then prioritize what's there and begin working through it to relieve the overwhelmed feeling and can manage my way through the rest of the clutter." Organzied people just seem to know what to do about it and take action. Clutterers may know what they are supposed to do, but taking action is the hard part.

"Cleaning Up" Doesn't Last

"Much of our business is repeat customers, both corporate and pri-vate. Very organized people call us once a year. Those who are disorga-nized call about twice a year," said Brian Scudamore, CEO and founder of 1-800-GOT-JUNK? (*www.1800gotjunk.com*), a franchise in 34 U.S. and Canadian cities. They haul clutter by the truckload from businesses and residences, recycling 60 percent. Their success is a testament to our clut-tered society. The notion that the disorganized call them back twice as often as the organized is strong proof that organizing the outside without tackling the deeper issues, is temporary.

What Hasn't Worked for Clutterers

Here are the most representative responses to my online survey:

1. Trying to create paper files for everything.

2. File trays **do not** work for me, no matter how many divisions there are.

3. I've tried setting aside special time, like a three-day weekend to clean up.

4. Putting all paperwork into three filing cabinets, in individual folders.

5. Seminars, books, temporary self-determination (usually brought on by a "suggestion" from the boss). Day planners which get lost in the stuff. I found one from 1984 with just two months used (Jan. and Aug.).

6. Putting everything onto my computer.

Why Haven't These Things Worked?

1. Not enough time in the day for "clerical" work.

2. I need a document to literally stare me in the face in order to act on it. Once it is laying flat and something else is on top, it might as well be on the moon.

3. I get caught up in an unimportant task I refer to as "Constructive Procrastination." So I spend time on it and neglect important projects.

4. I can't decide what to throw away, so I run out of room. Now all the folders are stuffed, and I need to clean them out yearly, which I have failed to do!

5. I might know, but can't begin to put it into words.

6. Scanning seems to be more trouble than it is worth.

What Has Worked

Martha, a first-level manager with a large telecommunications company, summed it up.

"I agree with writer Frederick Herzberg that intrinsic motivation in a job is more effective than extrinsic factors are. It has always worked for me to find some kind of meaning in my work. I think I have had above average success extending that to my staff."

Judith Kolberg, besides having written the ground-breaking book, *Conquering Chronic Disorganization* (Squall Press, 1999), is a career consultant who has worked with thousands of chronically disorganized people. Tailoring organizing systems based on a person's learning style is the key to her success. Some managers will cringe when they read this. "Do you mean we are going to have a hundred different organizing methods for a hundred employees? How will we keep control?" Ms. Kolberg's work has shown that this method works when others have failed.

Ms. Kolberg founded the National Study Group on Chronic Disorganization (*www.nsgcd.org*), which consists of Professional Organizers who specialize in innovative approaches for people who have not benefited from traditional organizing methods. I am deeply indebted to her and to her work. Many of my methods and insights are mirrored in her book. This provided validation that others are working along the same lines I am.

Her book was the first place I encountered the term "chronically disorganized," outside of my own writing.

Martha Swain asked the same question when managing hundreds of employees. "I think it is good for managers to be able to respect different styles of organization. As long as an individual or work group is effective, the style of organization should not be an issue. If a specific problem can be associated with lack of organization, it should be addressed. You find out if that is the case by being a good listener. A boss who is obsessed with looking good and having the workplace look good, without addressing these issues, will appear to be rearranging the deck chairs on the *Titanic*."

Let's Do an Inventory

When you know where you are, you can get where you want to go. Most of us are a little hazy about both.

Before we get into the psychological reasons behind our cluttering and how to change on the inner level, let's do a very practical inventory. A business that doesn't take a regular inventory doesn't know what to order and what to put on sale.

So it is with us. Our work and home lives are intertwined, so they are both represented. Take your time and think about your answers. You are making an investment in changing your life. Don't shortchange yourself.

Put the following charts into an 8 1/2 × 11 spiral notebook, with the pages laid out side-by-side. Put the first chart on the left page and the next one on the facing page. This is so you can glance from one to the other. I've chosen only five items per chart, for several reasons. While this is **your** game plan for change, please trust your coach.

Most tests have 10 questions. For clutterers, that's just too many. Five seems easy. Some of you will come want to expand this to 20 or more. Please resist the temptation.

 If you can get clarity with only five things and work on them right now, you are doing far more than you would overwhelming yourself with 20. When you've gotten five things under control, you can do this again. And again.

Don't over-think your answers, or try to come up with the perfect idea. Don't stop and think about how to prioritize the items. Let them flow from your brain to your hand. The order has no relevance. Don't forget to include any volunteer work you do. I believe strongly, like

Harvey Mackay and other business leaders, that giving back is part of living deliberately.

Step 1. Find out your strengths and weaknesses.

IN WHAT AREAS AM I ORGANIZED/NEAT?		IN WHAT AREAS AM I DISORGANIZED/MESSY?	
BUSINESS	PERSONAL	BUSINESS	PERSONAL

Personal: Do you have a hobby where you are organized or neat? Is your golf bag full of non-golf junk? Do you put your clubs lovingly away (unless you've had a bad round, in which case you probably throw them into a corner) in their proper place? Do you sew or crochet and put the fabric back into a basket? Do you have a model train or stamp collection that is always together so you can show it off to others? Is your car neat? If you routinely drive clients around, I bet it is. How about your kitchen? Do you do handyman projects and always clean your tools and return them to the tool shed when you are done?

Business: Do you show up for work on time or a little early? That shows that you can follow a "system." Organized people don't think this is a big deal, but for the chronologically-challenged, it is a major accomplishment. Do you complete **some** projects on time? Are some projects organized and filed correctly, while others are not? Is your computer or PDA organized? If there are personal projects that you like and are organized about, try turning your office projects into "hobbies."

Neatness counts!

Are you neatly groomed? This is more of a plus than you might think. Tom Sullivan is an Agency Leader with American General Financial Group with dozens of agents working for him. "I can tell if an agent is disorganized by the way he dresses. You see a guy walking around with his tie undone and wrinkled slacks and you'll find sloppy work."

Kim Hass told me, "Another boss was messy—how he dressed, his office, etc.—and he relied on his secretaries to keep him organized. Without those secretaries to keep him organized, he had no idea what to do."

These are just ideas to get started. The point is to stop concentrating on the negative and give ourselves credit for areas we haven't thought of. To truly change our disorganized habits, we have to change our way of thinking. Don't look at "getting organized" as a chore. Look at it as a new adventure. Don't look at clearing the clutter from your office as a distasteful punishment. See it as a treasure hunt.

Step 2. Why are you better in some areas than others?

Take the previous chart and place it side by side with the following one. Now you're ready to do something about the situation.

WHY DO I LIKE THESE ACTIVITIES?		WHY DO I DISLIKE THESE ACTIVITIES?	
BUSINESS	PERSONAL	BUSINESS	PERSONAL

Ideally, you'll notice a pattern. Common answers for the left column are: "A sense of pride." "It relaxes me." "I feel like it makes a difference in my life or others'."

The right column often looks like this: "I don't feel like it's really important." "I resent having to do such a mundane task." "I'm creative and this is a routine task." "I'm just not good at this sort of thing."

Step 3. Analyze the similarities/differences.

The same reasons apply to housework as to company reports. If you find you're doing tasks that bore you and contribute to disorganization, look for ways to channel that energy.

WHY DO I LIKE THESE ACTIVITIES?		WHY DO I DISLIKE THESE ACTIVITIES?	
BUSINESS	PERSONAL	BUSINESS	PERSONAL

Rather than tackling every organizing obstacle, see if someone else can do it. If you have a personal assistant, let him do the trivial things so you can work on what's more important to you. For those of us who don't have assistants, we **might** (depending on whether your corporate environment is more conducive to goldfish than sharks) be able to get a fellow employee to do this for us in exchange for our doing something they don't like to do. There is a real danger here, even if you and the co-worker work it out. If the boss doesn't understand, she might pass by your buddy's desk and get a little upset if he is doing **your** work. Make sure you aren't shooting yourself in the foot. The self-employed can get a high school or college student to handle routine chores while we concentrate on the Big Picture.

Step 4. Ten excuses for, and solutions for, procrastination.

Behind every excuse is the solution. Excuses are reasons that grew up to be delinquents. Let's teach those wayward excuses how to live productive, adult lives.

Excuse	Solution
1. It bores me.	1. Not everything we do has cosmic relevance. By letting petty tasks bother me, I give them more importance than they deserve. Set aside an hour a day to do boring tasks. Pick the hour before lunch, or the last hour of the day. Reward yourself for doing them. Eating or going home may be the best rewards some days.
2. It's just too overwhelming.	2. Sure, a huge task like going through a month's worth of mail or papers to file is overwhelming. Break it down into smaller tasks. An inch of mail, or papers to be filed. Even an earthworm can move an inch without straining himself. If he thought he had to cross a yard of ground, he too, would be overwhelmed. Inch by inch is a cinch.
3. There isn't enough time to finish, so I can't start.	3. How do you know that? The only way to find out is to start. If it is something that can be broken into smaller chunks, or delegated, then do it. If you don't start now, it will still take too long later.
4. I'd rather be doing something else.	4. Sure you would. I'd rather fish than clean out my filing cabinet. If I leave it undone and go fishing, it'll still be there when I get back. Do it and reward yourself by doing what you want when you've finished.
5. It is beneath me. I resent my boss for having assigned it to me in the first place.	5. If Mahatma Gandhi could clean toilets, you can do a menial task. Maybe you feel like you should be wearing a cap and a t-shirt with your company logo to do this. If you can express your feelings to your boss in a positive way, do it. If not, picture yourself as a fast-food worker and have fun with it. Wear a silly cap when you do silly tasks. If you don't do this thing, you won't advance from burger flipper to assistant manager.

Excuse	Solution
6. I'm just no good at this sort of thing. I don't have a head for figures, filing, organizing, etc.	6. Try to look at it in a different way. I hate to balance a checkbook, believing I am no good with numbers. But I love computers. I was a stock options trader. I loved the purity of numbers in a spreadsheet and on graphs. Find another way of approaching the thing you hate or combining it with something you love and do it differently. Do you like to draw? Then draw a filing system. Draw an organized office. Then make them reality.
7. I'm not really capable of doing this. I've worked myself up to my level of incompetency. Everyone will know what a dunce I am if I turn in a half-baked project.	7. Your boss thought you were capable of this. Is he a dunce? (Loaded question, I know.) What you're doing is not life or death. We grow by stretching. If you need to learn more to do your job, take classes. Read books. View this as a challenge to improve your life, not limit it. Most of us stop growing long before reaching our level of incompetence.
8. What difference will it make? If I do a good job, my boss will take the credit and if I do a lousy job, I'll get blamed.	8. If you do a good job, your boss will look good and you'll keep getting a paycheck. If you get blamed, will your paychecks stop? (See #7.) If you put it off too long, they might.
9. Why should I put a lot of effort into this? In this company we are always doing busy work. Management never follows up.	9. So? You can a) do a half-baked job since it doesn't matter anyway, b) get it out of the way so you can do something you like, or c) look for another job as soon as you finish this particular piece of busywork. Seriously, when you define what you don't like about your current position, you can make sure you don't jump into another similar situation.
10. I'm on the fast track. I won't be here in six months when this is supposed to be done, so what difference does it make if I spend time on it now?	10. None, if that is true. Except, when we have the attitude of doing as little as possible, it catches up with us somewhere. Do the best you can with what you have where you are. It will pay off in personal integrity. There are only so many six-month job jumps you can make. Something may happen at your current job that will make staying more attractive. Not having done a project six months ago may scuttle your chances for advancement.

Myths and Solutions

You already know how you're "supposed" to get organized. You've heard the same advice over and over. If it worked, you wouldn't be reading this. So what's wrong? You aren't dumb. In fact, disorganized people usually have higher than average intelligence (so why can't we just file a piece of paper?) and are creative.

Filing, organizing, and decluttering are boring. We would rather be expressing our creativity. We resent having to get organized. While I can't recall an incident where a disgruntled disorganized employee actually shot one of those pesky neat-freaks who make us clutterers look bad, we probably don't send them Holiday cards.

We should feel superior. While they are being good little soldiers, keeping their cubicles and offices in a Zen minimalist manner, we are creating the "next big thing" in our fantasy world—our imaginations. The poor things, they don't have the imagination and creativity we have. We should pray for them.

Unfortunately, our bosses may not be as spiritually elevated as we are, and might think that the neatness nuts should be lauded and promoted over us. Go figure. So, I guess we'd better get on their bandwagon. But we can do it without sacrificing any of our values.

I'll present traditional advice and interpret it so that clutterers can use it. Some traditional advice is correct and works for us. Most just makes us anxious.

Myth: Handle Each Piece of Paper Once

Solution: Most things cannot be resolved the first time we get them. If it can be resolved or delegated right away, then do it and be done with it. **Will it take less time to take care of this now rather than later?** If so, then you've got your answer. If not, file it.

We'll get into the intricacies of filing systems for different types of people soon, but the Big Concept here is that the sooner we take action on a paper, the sooner we can get rid of it for good. **Do something** with each piece of paper you handle. Move it along towards resolution or destruction. Tossing it back in your in-basket doesn't count. Neither does stuffing it into the middle of your Leaning Tower of Paper.

Myth: Make Your Doing List in 15 Minute Increments

Solution: Sure, this might work for busy executives with lots of appointments and a secretary. But most of us have more tasks to handle than people visiting us. Segmenting our day into 15-minute slots makes us feel like hamsters on a treadmill. Ease up. One 30-minute time-slot gives us the illusion of more than two 15 minute ones. Once you adapt to the "About" time system explained in Chapter 14, time won't bother you so much anymore.

Myth: Make a System and Follow It

Solution: This is a great idea—if **you** make **your** system. Tailor-make a system that works for you, based on your optimum learning style. Since it is yours, you have permission from the creator to adapt it to changing conditions.

Myth: Time Is the Same for Everyone

Solution: Clutterers don't relate well to clock-time. We miss deadlines because we hyperfocus (an ADD-like trait) and lose track of time. We are late for appointments because we get distracted.

Every business has timelines. Some of the strictest time-constrained businesses have apparently disorganized people working in them. **And** they meet the finish lines. Texas State Representative, Craig Eiland (D), is a very organized man. He keeps law offices in Houston and Galveston and a legislative office in the state capitol. "The legal field is much more strict and has more sanctions if you are not on time than most businesses do." In the legislature, time is crucial. If so many lawyers/legislators are apparently disorganized, how can they function in this profession? "**Inability to have reward is the motivating factor.** During the legislative session, your whole world is controlled by time. If you don't get your bill there in time, it won't be voted on. In a short period of time, the government clock is most important."

If the reward at work isn't motivating us, set up your own reward system to keep on track. Reward yourself with time when you do something on time. Take a day off when you finish a big project on time. Take an hour off when you get a few routine tasks done regularly on time after a week or so. Just getting our paycheck hasn't motivated us. Let's be our own best motivator.

This Is Only the Beginning

This is just a start on the road to getting permanently organized. We should have found out by now that:

▶ We are not all bad.

▶ We are organized in some areas and not in others.

▶ We have reasons for what we do or don't do.

We have laid enough foundation to get to the really important work of understanding why we do what we do and what we can do to change. I'm going to ask you to switch back to the theoretical in the next few chapters. Some of you won't want to. You will want to jump ahead to the chapters on better filing systems, time-management and stuff like that. I can't send Sister Mary My-Way-Or-The-Highway out to rap your hands with a ruler, but I can offer you these thoughts.

I used to skip to the "meat" of organizing and self-improvement books. Like Inspector Lestrade in the Sherlock Holmes mysteries, I considered myself a logical doer and thinker. He chided Mr. Holmes for being a "theorist." Facts solved cases, not theories.

Facts, without understanding what creates the situations, are only half the picture. Motivation causes behavior that makes the facts. We've got to understand the problem before we can tackle it. We need to know why.

Neat little tips and tricks haven't solved your problem before, long-term, have they? Techniques are tools. You can't pick up a scalpel and perform brain surgery just because you have a pretty good idea of where the brain is. It's generally better to know how the brain works, and what to cut out without destroying the whole thing.

Thus it is with this approach to learning to not clutter. Discover **why we do,** and the **how not to** will be easier.

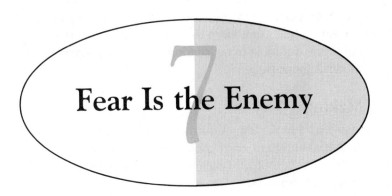

Fear Is the Enemy

*People who have this problem do have serious
problems making decisions and usually make many
bad ones because of their fears. We allow our minds to be as
cluttered as our offices, cars, and homes—adding to our
difficulty in making decisions.*

—Beth, a clutterer

Key Concepts

Our fears keep us from moving forward.

1. Fear of making a mistake (misplaced perfectionism).

2. Fear of making a decision.

3. Fear of changing the status quo.

4. Fear of failure.

5. Fear of success.

FEAR Is the Root of All

Non-cluttered people won't understand this chapter. Clutterers will. In my workshops, this segment gets the most "Ah-ha's." We don't need Freudian analysis to clear our desks, but we do need to understand why we made the clutter. This statement generated hundreds of e-mails from my *Dr. Laura* interview.

If you blame your poor filing habits on a fear of monsters in the filing cabinets, Freudian analysis may be called for. For most of us, the following are the common fears that keep us from getting organized. Not everyone has all of them, but most of us have one or two and have never related them to our disorganization.

Fear of Making a Mistake

You make 'em. I make 'em. Your bosses make 'em. We all make 'em. Letting fear of making them keep you cluttered is the biggest mistake you can make. Obsessing about mistakes when you make them is the second biggest mistake you can make.

We are perfectionists. One of the reasons we don't finish things, or don't do them in the first place is a fear that we will do them imperfectly (make a mistake). So, our "solution" is to do nothing, or do one insignificant project perfectly, ignoring the Bigger Picture.

How Did You Learn to Drive?

You didn't learn to drive without getting some instruction from someone. You didn't just jump in, turn the key, and roar down the Santa Monica Freeway. (Although, I have been behind several people who drive that way) It took a series of small decisions, learning, and making mistakes before we hit the road.

Our fear of making mistakes is tied up with our self-esteem. We see people we admire or envy doing things right, and we think they always do things right. We feel inferior to them, because we only see the results. We don't see the process. And we are acutely aware of our own processes.

But What if I Throw Out Something Important?

Most information:

▶ Is available somewhere else.

▶ Can be recreated.

▶ Isn't that important.

What do we do when we throw away the only copy of a file that **was** important, delete the e-mail with the valuable information, and present a proposal based on faulty information?

Don't worry; you'll learn some tools that will protect you.

The next chapter teaches decision-making skills, but since fear is what keeps you from making them, stop worrying right now. There's a backup method that prevents you from making irrevocable mistakes. Stop dwelling on your mistakes. Just because you make a mistake doesn't mean you are a failure. Your self-esteem is more than your job performance.

The safe path is not to make any decisions, never to throw anything out. So our Shadow Self, our cluttered self, tells us. But it is lying. When our files and Doing lists are so cluttered that we can't use them, it's like trying to get a dress or shirt out of a closet stuffed with every piece of clothing you've every owned. It's there, but it's not available.

If you can't find it, it might as well not exist.

So it is when we don't declutter our desks, files, and computers. Information is useless if it isn't available. We make more mistakes because we can't find something in the clutter, than we will make by decluttering.

That important file may be hidden in a 12-inch stack of file folders, but if we really needed it, we would no more be able to find it than if we had shredded it.

You cannot do everything perfectly.

Perfectionism is protectionism. If we never finish anything, we can always say we are working on it. The next time you get a small project, like the menu for the company picnic, try this exercise to break that habit. Don't try it with your annual budget review, the designs for a new space shuttle, or your boss's European schedule.

Decide how long you need to spend on it. Cut off one-quarter of that time. When three-quarters of the time is gone, review it. Finish it on time. Read it over once. Correct any errors. Let it go. We spend too much time "perfecting" things that don't need or deserve the attention we give them. Redoing them five times "improves" things that don't need fixing. Trust yourself to do it as right as you can the first time, allow yourself a once-over, and be done with it.

Fear of Making Decisions

If we don't make decisions, we don't make mistakes. We keep every paper that crosses our desk, even though we know we couldn't find it if we needed it. Just knowing it is there makes us feel like we have covered ourselves.

We **have** covered ourselves, the same way a gravedigger covers a grave. Visualize each piece of paper as another shovelful of dirt on your career grave. Keep on doing what you've always been doing and you'll keep getting the same results.

You already know how to make decisions. You just don't give yourself credit for making them. By not making a decision on the importance of what to keep and what not to keep, you've made a decision. You're making decisions. You're just making the wrong ones.

How many decisions have you already made today?

You decided to go to work today. You decided what clothes to wear. You decided to drive, take a bus or a train. You decided what time to leave. You decided to…. You see, before you even sat down at your desk, you've made a dozen or more decisions. And they were all good ones.

If you drive, you make big decisions every day. You could decide that it's just too overwhelming to see all that traffic in your rear-view mirror, so you could start changing lanes without looking and eventually suffer drastic consequences. But you don't, because the perceived consequences of not making a decision are too great.

So it is with work. The decision not to make any decisions portends a career wreck in your future.

Today, it's unlikely that your work decisions will threaten the lives of people around you. You could have caused a 50-car pileup on the freeway today. You didn't, I hope. One thing I've learned from putting statements on paper or speaking to groups is that there will invariably be someone who will say, "As a matter of a fact, I did." When speaking about the fear of not being needed, I say that we often act as if we are the information officer at a library. Having others ask us for information makes us feel needed. A lady raised her hand at a workshop and said, "As a matter of a fact, I **am** the information desk person at a library." For her, being needed was part of her job. She didn't need to bring that insecurity home.

You Are Not Your Decisions

"Be process-oriented rather than goal-oriented. A good example is someone who is looking for a job. When they focus on whether they get a job that day they get demoralized and it affects their self-image. If they shift to how many letters they sent out and how many people got their resumes, that's better," explains Dr. Terrence S. Early, MD, Associate Professor, Department of Psychiatry and Behavioral Sciences and Director of Research for the Psychiatry Department at Univ. of Texas Medical Branch.

You are not the result of your decisions. The process of making them ends your personal involvement. Trust yourself to create and follow intelligent processes. If the results are what you want, the process worked. If they aren't, either the process needs to be modified or it's due to factors beyond your control. In the previous example, you made the correct decision (send out resumes). The results are affected by conditions outside your control (the mail got lost, the job was already filled, the personnel manager hired his brother, it wasn't the right job for you). If don't get the results you expect, reevaluate the process (is your resume weak, are you looking in the wrong places, if there another process that would be more efficient)? Either way, the results are the consequences of taking action, based on the process, but independent from your inner self. Once you learn to separate the process from the results, it will be easier to make decisions.

It's as if efficient people stand behind a window observing their decisions and the results. Efficient people look at the results, but the results are separate from their self-image. When they don't get the results they expect, they adjust the process. They don't let them ruin their self-esteem. They are not their decisions.

Clutterers smash the window, so each result affects our self-image. Our reactions ricochet off the pavement and hit our inner selves with feelings of success or failure. If the results are "good" we are up. If the results are "bad," we are down. If we keep that glass shield between the results and our inner self, we can observe the results and learn from them, but not let them put us on an emotional roller coaster.

Fear of Changing the Status Quo

Your life is working now. It's not working very well, but at least you know what it's like. If you make the decision to change it, it could be uncomfortable. When people believed the world was flat, it was comfortable because it was all they knew. When Columbus disproved it, the entire world had to shift and change. It caused dis-ease.

Columbus made a decision. He decided that he could achieve fame and fortune (his Big Picture) by finding India (the Goal). He thought he could do that by sailing west (the Process). He was wrong about where he was going and how to get there, yet he achieved his Big Picture goals of fame and fortune (for a time anyway, such are the rewards of transient goals), even though he made a slight error in judgment. He maintained to the end that he had reached Asia. He, too, was afraid to admit he had made a mistake.

You are like Columbus. You are embarking on a journey to find peace and success. Though most of your shipmates will be happy for you, there will be a few who will try to hold you back. Columbus's crew tried mutiny because they were fearful. Your coworkers, and sometimes, your family may have fears they don't want to confront, too. They liked the old you, the fearful you. They could manipulate you. You weren't a threat to the status quo. When they realize that you could move ahead of them on the ladder of success, they may try to hold you back. They could try mutiny by making fun of your efforts. They will tell you that the world really is flat and you are a crazed captain. They will tell you that you need to turn back now, before you kill them all and sail off the edge of the earth.

Besides your human counterparts, you have a whole crew within you: Shadow Selves (Chapter 13), self-limiting beliefs, basic insecurities. I'm going to make suggestions to help you change your life. It won't be as hard as you fear. Believe in yourself. Belief and fear cannot coexist. (No, this is not the part where you should stand up and shout, "I believe! Hallelujah! I beeeeeiiilllliiieeeevve. That usually happens around Chapter 14).

Fear of Failure

A couple of apparent failures team up.

Abraham Lincoln's greatest ally was another seeming failure. General Ulysses S. Grant was perhaps a bigger failure than Lincoln. He wasn't very good as a military man in his early career. He resigned his commission because of the fear of being disgraced. He was a rotten businessman. He had bad luck. He once tried to grow crops on a bend in the Columbia River, when stationed at Fort Vancouver, Oregon. The land was good. Potatoes were expensive—16 cents a pound. Grant thought he was going to make lots of money. The river flooded. He had made a bad decision—a mistake. He made many, but a fellow officer, Colonel Thomas Anderson, said, "I never knew any man that showed such growth as General Grant showed. I am convinced he became a great general because he went through the tortures of the damned during his frontier service in California and the Oregon territory."

Grant's letters are full of insecurities. He resigned his commission and tried civilian life. After failing at farming and real estate, he was working at his father's hardware store when the Civil War started. He scrambled to get into the war. Other military leaders thought little of him. He was probably an active alcoholic by today's standards (though there are some who dispute this). General Robert E. Lee was probably smarter than Grant. He graduated second in his West Point class, compared to General Grant's standing as 21st out of 29.

President Lincoln was a tortured man. General Grant was an insecure man, propped up by an enormous ego. Together, they were full of insecurities. Together, they changed history. These two apparent failures and weaklings made tough decisions and correct ones. They kept on keeping on. Why?

Lincoln believed in something. He believed in something greater than himself. He was part of what he believed in, but not all of it. He believed he could add something to the human experience. Grant believed in himself. Lincoln believed in Grant. He saw within him the greatness that others missed.

They experienced failure after failure. They kept trying, adjusting the processes until they got it right. They knew what they wanted; they just had to figure out how to get there. It's the same with you. You're going to "fail" at organizing sometimes. You're going to "fail" at making decisions. It doesn't matter how many "failures" you have—they don't make *you* a failure. It's the process that failed, not you. You can keep tinkering with the process until you get it right.

You didn't just wake up this morning cluttered. You've been this way for a long time. Thinking you can overcome a major challenge like this in "X" number of days if self-defeating. You can get better right now, today. You can keep getting better almost every day. You'll have setbacks, but you'll never slide back to where you started. You'll always have one foot on the road to self-improvement.

Fear of Success

Many of us are afraid of being found out, that we are really incompetent, that we are frauds. If we blame our mistakes on not being able to find things, we at least have a scapegoat. If we document everything, we feel there might be mistakes made by others in those papers that we can point to when things go awry.

Bill E. Vice-President of a medium-sized manufacturer told me his story:

"I graduated from a small college, with only a Bachelor's degree. I was good at sales and was consistently the top performer. I got promoted to district sales manager and ultimately to upper management. I liked being a salesman, meeting people, talking to them and finding ways to help them. But, a promotion had its benefits too, and besides, everyone told me I'd be crazy to turn it down.

"At first it seemed to fit in with my long-term goals. Working at the corporate office enabled me to spend more time at home with my family. Plus, the money was good.

"Everything went fine for a few years. I got promoted three times. The higher I went, the more complex were the tasks that were assigned to me. I got more memos. More paper crossed my desk, all of it seemingly important.

"I felt like I spent all my time doing paperwork, much of it duplicated or meaningless. Instead of talking to customers, I rarely talked to anyone outside my department.

"I had several secretaries. Each time I got a new one, I had to explain what I wanted. Finally, I realized I didn't know what I wanted. I wanted less paper on my desk, but I couldn't convey to my secretary how to make that happen.

"Most of my peers had higher degrees from more prestigious institutions. I always felt they looked down on me. Some of the managers below me had better credentials. I felt like they were wolves, circling, just waiting for me to show weakness, before they pounced for the kill.

"At first, I could delegate parts of projects, but then I started to fear that the other person would do something wrong, and I wouldn't catch it, or that he would somehow get all the credit. So I tried doing everything myself.

"That meant making more decisions. I was terrified that, if I made a wrong decision, I'd be pilloried at a meeting. So, I would delegate, then take the project back, or not give my subordinate all the relevant information. I figured I could maintain control that way. Then, if I presented it, and it was incomplete, I could always blame it on someone else.

"That worked pretty well. But now, I'm afraid that I'll get caught, or ratted out by one of the wolves below me. My home life has gone downhill and I actually spend more time at the office now than at home. Even the simplest things are hard to decide, so I spend an inordinate amount of time on trivial matters. I feel like a hamster on a treadmill."

I've Got the Guilts and I Don't Know Why

We all have "shoulds" that tug at us. We should take that promotion. We should have a family. We should make more money. We should be perfect.

If we get all these things and don't find happiness and fulfillment, we feel guilty about what we *do* have; about what we **have** achieved. We even feel guilty about not feeling **grateful** for what we have.

Maybe we "should" find ourselves. How much money is enough? How many promotions will it take for us to feel like we've "arrived?" Were we really happier when we were single? Simplifying our lives will simplify our clutter. Maybe our work goals and our personal goals are in conflict. The angst list is endless. The vague anxieties roll in an endless tape.

We work best (and clutter less) when we work at a job that fits us. Bill was happier as a salesman. He liked talking to people. He may even have liked traveling, and not spending every night with his family. "Typical" family life isn't for everyone. An advanced degree isn't as much of a corporate "oughta" for a successful salesman. A salesman's results are quantifiable. Being in a position where everyone else has more letters behind their names can make you feel like an imposter.

When We Are Driven by Fear, It's a Long, Lonely Road

Let's stop the fear train. Until we do, we will use disorganization as an ineffectual method of coping. As long as we have our cluttering to blame, we don't have to take responsibility. As long as we can shuffle papers, we can feel like we are doing something, when we are really afraid to tackle meaningful projects because we feel incompetent. Traditional management advice is to surround ourselves with people more competent than we are. If we're scared of getting found out, we aren't likely to put spies in our own camp.

We probably aren't as bad as we think. Managers above us wouldn't be likely to keep promoting us if we were—unless they are also insecure and only promote those they can control.

Ask yourself a few questions and take time to think about the answers.

1. Do I feel fearful in other aspects of my life?

2. Have I always felt this way?

3. If not, when did it start and what changed?

4. Do I have one or more thing(s) that I seem to do well at work?

5. Do I have one or more things that I seem to do well in my personal life?

6. Did I seem this disorganized when I was in another position?

We can't clean up our cluttering habits until we clean up our emotions. What we do at work may be an escape valve for our unresolved inner issues. While consulting a psychiatrist or psychiatric counselor to get organized may seem like shooting a fly with an elephant gun, remember—**it isn't about your stuff. It's about your relationship with your stuff.** You may be using your disorganization to protect you from your own feelings of inadequacy.

In the personal arena, this is often manifested by clutterers imagining that their stuff defines them; that it somehow protects them from an uncertain future. In our business lives, we can just quantify it better. Look—you've got a problem. You need a solution. In your business life, you don't hesitate to bring in experts and consultants. Sometimes the experts can't solve your problem. They don't know where you are coming from, because they haven't been there. I have. The exception seems to be ADD career counselors. Often *they* have ADD.

Most of us are self-aware enough to make the required changes without professional help, once we understand the problem. Sometimes we just need a little light shone on a dark area in our psychological closet that we've been avoiding.

No matter what course of action you take, take some action.

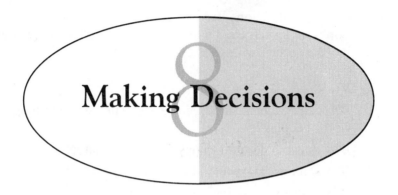

Making 8 Decisions

People with difficulty in making decisions, especially those with ADD and depression, have an overestimation of the danger involved. They have a vague idea about what will happen if they throw something out.

—Dr. Terrence S. Early MD, Psychiatrist

Key Concepts

1. How important is it?

2. The four Whys and Why Nots.

3. The time allotted to make a decision should be no more than the value of the outcome.

4. If you make 100 right decisions, the 101st may be wrong. But it is more likely to be right because you have confidence in your decision-making ability.

5. If the 101st is wrong, remember the first 100 and learn from the 101st.

Adults spend an average of 16 times as many hours selecting clothes (145.6 hours a year) as they do planning their retirement. We spend more time, proportionally, on deciding whether to file a paper than we do on buying a house. It's not the gravity or the complexity of a decision that determines its perceived value to us. It's the immediacy. By procrastinating, we make simple decisions become complex ones, but we could be worse. Ten books on a shelf can be arranged in 3,628,800 different ways. (For facts like this, visit *www.uselessknowledge.com*).

The Four Whys

1. *Why* can't we make a decision about whether something is worth keeping?
2. *Why* do we hold onto things that are outdated?
3. *Why* can't we just wade in and get rid of stuff?
4. *Why* do we keep doing the same things?

The Four Why Nots

1. *Why not* accept that we will make mistakes and go on?
2. *Why not* accept that we can decide what to keep and what to toss?
3. *Why not* accept that we didn't make this mess in one day and won't get rid of it in one day?
4. *Why not* start a new life—today?

General Guide to Making a Decision

Philosophers and economists tell us that we make decisions based on our Subjective Expected Utility or SEU. Will the end result make me feel good or satisfied? To make a "good" decision, we have to determine if we will be happy with the result. That's why it's hard.

There is a branch of psychology called behavioral decision theory that deals specifically with decision-making. You don't need a PhD to make a decision or understand this chapter. It should be reassuring to know that people have to go to school to learn how to make decisions, so don't feel poorly about yourself because you weren't born knowing how to make perfect decisions.

Making a decision is seldom a perfectly logical experience. Every decision we make is somehow related to our previous decisions. We create assumptions based on previous decisions of a similar nature. An excellent book on making decisions is *Decisions, Decisions: The Art of Effective Decision Making,* by David A. Welch.

Trust Your Instincts

These tools and rules are invaluable when getting started in learning how to make decisions. We, chronically disorganized people, don't trust our gut feelings because we don't feel confident about ourselves to begin with. After we start making some decisions and feeling good about the process, we can open up to our intuition. If the "rules" say to throw something out, and your gut says, "Wait a minute. I can't explain it, but I think we should keep this," then go with your gut. The most important tool you'll ever have is your gut.

When I first started to live a less cluttered life, I couldn't trust my instinctive reactions because my nature was to keep everything. Now that I have been on this path for a few years, I can trust my instincts.

There are at least five ways to make a decision. If you've been stuck using just one decision-making paradigm, maybe that's why what you're doing isn't working.

Optimization. This requires the most information and takes the most time to gather all the information. Generally, you would save it for really, really big decisions such as buying a house or car or changing careers, which require the most knowledge about the choices. For example, you'd use this when there are several facts and preferences that would affect your decision. You would assign them weights or values to arrive at the most logical decision. I mention it because we unknowingly use it when making trivial decisions like what to throw away. Don't get bogged down with decluttering.

Constrained optimization. This is what we will mostly deal with. You set limits on the process, "I must decide this within an hour." "I must keep all documents that begin with 'Dear So-called Customer Service." Those are the constraints you put on what to do. A decision that could go into this category or the following is like this: I have to fly to New York tomorrow and be there by 10 a.m. I want to use an airline that I have a frequent flyer account with, and get the best price and arrival time."

Satisficing. When you have alternatives that you don't know much about, this works more rapidly than optimization. You select the first option that is satisfactory since more information would be meaningless to you. For example: "I have to fly to New York tomorrow and be there by 10 a.m. Since I get frequent-flyer miles on any airline by using my credit card, and the cost is immaterial, it doesn't matter which airline I choose. I'll pick the first flight I can get." If cost is important, you would switch to constrained optimization, using the constraints of arrival times and cost.

Pre-selection. This is the easiest way to make a decision. It is also the most limited. If you have pre-selected certain criteria, you immediately eliminate those courses of action that don't fit. For example, if your Big Picture goal is to spend more time with your family, you apply the pre-selected criteria of "I will only look for jobs that do not require travel." However, once you have pre-selected six jobs that meet your criteria, you still have to choose one. At that time, you would switch mental gears and use optimization. However, if your criteria were sufficiently strict, they could eliminate the need for further decision-making. If you added the constraints: "A job must also pay more than $60,000 a year, be within a 20-minute commute, and in the entertainment industry," then there will be few selections.

In the airline example, you would say, "I will only fly Delta or United. I will arrange the meeting time to fit the airline schedule." Thus the pre-selection has been made and the time of arrival is unimportant.

It could be a good strategy for developing habits of filing. For example, you make a rule that all letters, faxes, memos relating to a project you are currently working on go into a hot file on your desk labeled "Project I am working on now." When the project is over, then you would have to switch to optimization to decide what to do with the files.

Randomization. It is rather unlikely that you will need this for anything in this book, except later as a tool. Briefly, it comes into play when you have to decide among many choices about which you have no feeling, and with absolute fairness. If you ever get tapped to determine the rules in an office pool, you can pull this out of your hat and look like a hero.

You'd use this in a situation in which you have no vested interest in the outcome and must remain impartial. You would be completely unattached to the outcome, but have to consider every relevant piece of information to make a decision. It's similar to doing statistical analysis. Your job would be to gather the data and let the data determine the decision.

Let's Put This Into Practical Applications

Now that you have some strategies to use, you have to apply tools. The first is *elimination by aspect*, technical talk for eliminating those things that just won't work. You do this every day. To get to work takes an hour by car. You could ride your bicycle, but it wouldn't be practical. You have just eliminated by aspect!

You can't spend your whole working day thinking about every little step you take. But just like learning to walk, you have to begin one baby step at a time. By the time you are 30 or 40 years old, you can probably walk without thinking about it.

Making Decisions Frees Us

We spend more time deciding which brand of toilet paper to get than on things that affect our career. Yet, after we have agonized over the 20 or so choices of size, brand, and color, we buy something and then don't think about it again. We don't put the decision on hold and go home, saying, "I'll get to it tomorrow." I've narrowed my choices a bit, by only buying white. An ecologically aware girlfriend once gave me a look that could have shriveled me like a prune when I bought colored paper. It's always stuck with me. Why would I remember that and forget important things? Read the chapter on memory and it will become clear that we remember visual, emotional things better than abstract things.

Once we've left the store, we don't think about it again. **Making a decision and accepting the outcome frees us. Not making a decision puts us in bondage to it.** (Okay, I recently grabbed the first package I saw. It turned out to be one-ply instead of the two-ply kind I've apparently always bought. After all, two is always better than one, isn't it? I didn't like it. But, I swear that's the only time I've ever given much thought to toilet paper, once bought).

We can learn two things from the previous examples:

1. Narrowing choices, even a little bit, eliminates a step in the process.

2. Impulsively deciding something without any thought at all isn't the answer.

Only Two Kinds of Decisions

Even a clutterer can handle two choices without getting bogged down.

1. Is it really, really major?

2. If it isn't, why am I spending so much time on it?

Aagh! Math

Car dealers told me that the average new car contract is 55 months or 236 weeks. A mortgage runs 30 years. That car purchase will be with you for about 1,670 days. A house will haunt you for 10,950 days and nights. What percentage of time do you spend on deciding each?

Though people generally buy a new car within two weeks of going to a dealer, they spend more time before they walk in the door researching and comparing cars. I spent four months. Let's assume you are more normal than I, and spent most of two weekends driving to dealers, and an hour a night reading ads, researching specs and annoying your spouse with the results of your search. ("You'll know it's time to stop researching when your significant other shouts at you, "I don't care if you get a Honda or a Humvee. Just buy the damn thing!"). Based on the above theory, assume you spent about 38 hours, almost a week of work time deciding on a new car.

Let's see, $5/1670 = 0.32$ percent. That's how much of the lifetime of an object we put into making a decision about it. A house is a bigger decision, and thus takes more of our time. Realtors say the average time to decide on a house is six weeks. If you spend four hours a weekend driving to properties and back, and two hours a night looking at ads or comparing mortgages, that's about 90 hours or 11 working days. $11/10950 = 0.10$ percent.

So, as a general rule of thumb, if we are spending more than 0.3 percent of our time in life on anything, it must be really, really important.

Let's Apply This to the Office

Surveys have shown that the average office worker receives 45 documents a day. Say we spend a minute on each deciding whether to file or toss it. We put it on our desk. We spend another minute a day looking at it, thinking we ought to file it. We spend 20 minutes looking for it a week later, because it turned out to be important. That's an hour for a piece of paper. Let's assume the same 40-hour workweek. Gosh, that's $1/40 = 2.5$ percent. Since we can't estimate the length of time a paper "lasts," unlike a car loan, (80 percent of them are never referred to again), we'll just stop with the amount of our work life it steals from us.

That innocuous-looking parchment must be more important than a $30,000 car or a $150,000 house! If we are paid for a 40-hour workweek (even if we work 60), for 50 weeks, that means you work about 2,000 hours a year. (I hope you get two weeks vacation). If we make $40,000 a year, that's about $20 an hour. Thus, each and every paper we agonize over costs us a brand new, crisp portrait of Andrew Jackson. If we make $100,000 a year, we're getting closer to making Ulysses S. Grant our paperweight. As you'll recall, he was not a good example of someone who made consistently good decisions.

The next time a paper crosses your desk, keep track of the time you spend on it. I asked several people to do this and they were amazed. My figures are actually on the low end, for clutterers.

We've put relatively minor things in the really, really important class. We are letting our indecision cost us real money.

So If It's Not Really, Really Important, What Do I Do?

Ask yourself one question:

What's the worst that will happen if I make a mistake?

Most of the time we don't know for sure. That's why we can't make a decision in the first place. We've assigned a scenario something like this to every decision.

"If I don't file it correctly, I won't be able to find it when it is needed. My boss will get upset. I will lose my job. I won't be able to find another. My unemployment will run out. I will be denied welfare. I'll end up on the street with a tin cup."

Let's try this instead:

Can I take action now that will avoid negative consequences?

According to decision experts, this is the short form of the Disaster Avoidance Principle. You want to do the thing that will cause you the least amount of harm. It's the conservative way to go.

In the case of a letter, the scenario would look something like this.

The myth of handling a piece of paper "just once" · we get it the first time for normies. Many things cannot be resolved. Hah! This doesn't even work

I CAN:

1. Answer it. File or destroy the original.

2. Make notes about it and file or destroy it.

3. Delegate it to someone who can do something about it.

4. Put it in a tickler file to be dealt with later.

5. Determine it is irrelevant. Destroy it.

Note that we didn't assign a great value to this letter. Its importance is the same as any other letter. There are only four possible things to do about it, and doing any of them gets it off your desk. While #1 and #2 are irrevocable, you are still covered, because you've summarized the contents. Some industries have to keep more paper than others: doctors, lawyers, accountants, insurance offices. Even if you have to keep the letter for backup, enter the cogent parts in a contact manager or database, so you can find what you need, even if you misfile it. The only time the original is important is if you get sued. If that happens, I bet you'll find the document, no matter how long it takes. At that point, it jumps into the really, really important category.

A Gambler's Odds

Making a real decision is a gamble. The only irrevocable, out-there-swinging-in-the-breeze action is #5. Even here, the odds are on our side. Most of the documents (80 percent) we get are never referred to again. Even if we throw something away that is valuable, the odds are better than any game in Las Vegas or in the Stock Market. It's best to start making small bets, like throwing away junk mail and catalogs before we jump in and lay big money down on the Pass line. But, as we learn to decide what is really important, we hedge our bets by knowing we can make decisions.

Paper Clutter Represents More Than You Think

Or so we think now. We can move beyond that. Before we deal with the papers, let's explore some of the insecurities the papers represent and banish them. They are literally paper tigers. Let's make 'em toothless pussycats.

The problem is our way of looking at the papers. The pile of papers is intimidating because we have imagined it as a minefield that could sink our careers.

Traditional advice tells us, "All you have to do is to start with the piece of paper at the top of your pile and work your way down. Once you've gotten rid of it, and implemented a system, you won't let it pile up again."

That might work for organized people. We clutterers have to overcome our feelings to do even the simplest tasks. We know logically that "all we have to do" is to set up a filing system and be religious about putting stuff into it. Once a year, or once a month, we know that we should go through it and purge it. Gee, how simple is that?

Changing Habits

We can change the habits of not-filing or not-eliminating papers to those of putting them in their place, literally. We can learn to treat them as papers, not life-threatening decisions. Our lives will be freer if we put parts of it on automatic pilot and save our decision-making muscles for when they are really needed.

How long will it take to change your paper hoarding habit? You may feel so great after the first couple of days of doing it that you switch gears right away. More likely, it will take months. And you may slip back into old behaviors. I don't like "X number of days to (the perfect office, the perfect body, the perfect relationship)." You are an individual. I don't care how many other people do something in "X" amount of time. You'll take as long as it takes—for you.

Deciding What Papers or E-mails to Keep

This works for paper clutter and e-mail clutter. Copy this prescription and tape it (it's going to have to stay there for awhile) to the top of your computer. If you have to take down a cartoon to make room, it's worth the sacrifice. Keep the note there until these four steps are habits. I hope one day to be touring an office and see half the computers with this four-point plan stuck to them:

1. Is it outdated?

2. Is it relevant to my projects?

3. Can it be summarized?

4. Does it still have to be filed?

You'll need four tools to accomplish this task: a highlighter, a pair of scissors, a computer open to your contact manger or database, and a trash basket or shredder. Get all that ready before you start, because once you start, you do not want to take a break.

Inch-by-Inch Is a Cinch

Getting through that whole pile is overwhelming. Break it down into one-inch piles. First, though, flip the stack upside down. The older something is (ourselves excluded), the less likely it is to have value. It's easier to see that outdated things don't have value. Once we realize this, we can keep things that will become outdated from piling up.

Now you have several one-inch stacks, arranged archeologically. Before you begin, visualize your desk clear and clutter-free (If visualization is new to you, see Chapter 12 for specifics).

Make It a Treasure Hunt, Not a Chore

First, change your attitude towards the piles. **This is not a chore. It is a treasure hunt.** You will find things you've forgotten about, things that have real value among the junk. That's an immediate payoff.

Now, ask yourself, "If this whole messy pile were to burn up, how much difference would it make?" Would your company go bankrupt? Would you lose your job? Would my worth as a person be lessened?

You have desensitized the piles. They are just papers. They aren't the future of our company. They have nothing to do with your worth as a person.

1. Is it outdated?

Grab that first piece of paper. Scan it visually. Is there a date on it? That should put in into perspective. Look for a "reply by" date. Has it passed? If so, discard it immediately, without reading. It is outdated and of no value. Even if it says you could have been promoted to Executive Vice-President-in-Charge-of-Everything, it is too late to do anything about it. Trash the paper.

If it's not outdated, highlight the date and proceed to step two.

If there is no date, go to step two.

2. Is it relevant?

Look at the heading to see if it's from a supplier or customer you still work with. If not, pitch it. If it's a memo, is the person who wrote it still with the company? See if you can divine the message without having to read the whole thing. That's another key. Most of what is written (except this book, of course) is fluff. Seldom is business writing as terse as the writer thinks it is.

If it begins with "First of all, let me thank (express, put into words) etc.," you can probably skip the first paragraph. Sure it is nice that the writer is thanking us for taking the time from our busy schedule or is concerned about the welfare of our family, but do we really care at this point?

Paper. When you see key words that make this document relevant, highlight them on papers. Sample words are "key," "relevant," "price," "satisfaction," "dissatisfaction," "sue," "award," "broken (usually followed by 'promises' or 'your product'), "pay," "##XX!!!??!!" (While the last set of expletives is not important in itself, it might be a flag that you should read the whole thing.)

Be aware that some writers go on forever, in an attempt to lull you into a false sense of security, then throw in a "gotcha." Look out for changes in thoughts signaled by "however," "but," "on the other hand," and "erroneous." If the writer typed "erogenous" instead, don't read anything into it.

E-Mail: If you use Outlook, you can click "Edit Message," then find the relevant phrases and apply a boldface font or even a new color if you want. You can also delete text, which moves you into step three. Outlook Express doesn't have a feature to do this.

3. Can it be summarized?

Paper: With the highlighted text being all you really need, note the entry as the date of the letter, type the important stuff into your contact manager and discard the paper, unless you need it for a CYA file.

E-Mail: Cut and paste the relevant info into your contact manager. Be sure to date the entry according to the date of the e-mail, not today's date. The temptation here is to keep the e-mail. If you already have (or have entered) the person's e-mail address and have entered the relevant information, you don't need the e-mail anymore. You just have to be ruthless with e-mails or they will pile up and bite you later.

4. Does it still have to be filed?

Oh my God! Now you really have to make a decision. Up until now, you've just been storing stuff or eliminating things that were obviously irrelevant.

STOP RIGHT THERE!

You **have** made a number of decisions. Give yourself credit for having done that. You've decided what was important. You've decided to put that information into a place where you'll be able to find it. You were able to do these things because none of them were irrevocable. You still had the paper in front of you, just in case you made a mistake.

Now we will get into the most important part of this exercise—learning to trust yourself to make good decisions.

Trust Yourself

Go back and read the relevant information you put into your contact manager. Compare it with the whole document. Don't worry, you won't have to do this for every document for the rest of your life. But first, to learn to trust yourself, you will.

Did what you entered really seem to summarize the document? If your boss called you tomorrow, could you refer to this computer file and give her the information needed? If you can truthfully answer "yes" to those two questions, you could get rid of the paper or e-mail right now.

You see, you have filed it, at least what was important. That's another key concept. A filing cabinet is an extension of our memories. If we all had photographic memories, we wouldn't need to keep books, tapes, or files. Since we don't, we "file" some sort of hanger that will prompt us to go to a paper file to find something. Chapter 9 elaborates on filing systems.

I'm going to propose a general purpose filing technique here. Your exact filing system will depend on what kind of learner you are, covered in the next chapter. The following idea will work for anyone.

Create a Safety Net

If throwing something away right now is too hard for you, lighten up.

Paper: Let's make a "What If" file. Create a hanging file for the front of your filing cabinet (but not on your desk) labeled "What if." Within it, make manila files, one per month. Remember to put the month and year on the upper right-hand corner.

E-Mail: Create a directory in your e-mail program called "What If." Under that, make subdirectories for several months. Move the e-mails and attachments you've summarized into the month folder.

Sure, this is not getting rid of your clutter. Sure, it flies in the face of what you may have read elsewhere. Think of it as training wheels for a bicycle. First you learn to ride the bike, to coordinate your feet with the pedals, your hands with the brakes and gears. Then you have to try to avoid getting run over by big, mean old cars. That's a lot of stuff to do. If you add the danger of falling down and getting skinned up to the mix, it may just be too overwhelming.

It's the same here. Just because we went through a process once in the exercises above, doesn't mean they have taken root in our subconscious. We have to go through them time and time again, until we are comfortable with them. We aren't changing our filing systems. We are changing our lives. A therapist doesn't listen to you once, give you a sheet of paper with exercises to do at home and pronounce you cured. You have to go back again and again. Sometimes you have to cover the same ground. Sometimes you feel like you've mastered a new behavior, or completely eliminated an old one and surprise!

An Extra File?

What's the harm in having an extra file? Before you started to make these changes in your life, you had all that old paper junking up your desk or files anyway. You've summarized them so that you can find them easily. If you keep them for a month or two longer, the world will not end. You will not be a weakling. You will not have failed.

Keeping the old stuff will make it easier to move forward. If you've eliminated the fear factor, there are fewer reasons to "not clutter." You will also build up your decision-making muscles by making decisions. True, you will know that your backup is always there, in case you make a mistake. But, as more time goes on, and you find you don't have to refer to your backup, you'll feel more confident. You'll learn to trust yourself.

If You Backslide, Don't Panic

How many times have you gone on a diet, tried to quit smoking, tried to learn a new language, a new hobby? How many times did you get it right the first time and never falter, never give up? Never? Aw, come on, be serious.

If people with life-threatening diseases like diabetes, alcoholism, obesity, or drug addiction can sometimes slip back into old behaviors, why should we think we won't. For them, the consequences are huge—death. For us, it's just a minor setback. Remember that when you get discouraged.

The old behavior pops back up, perhaps stronger than before. You get tired of doing things "right" and slip back into the old ways. You feel like you've backslid. This is going to happen with your business life. At the very least it's going to take months to change for good. At the worst, it's going to take a year or so.

What About That What-If Folder

After you've developed a comprehensive filing system based on the next few chapters and used it for enough time to feel confident, you can go to the "What If" files and throw away the oldest file. When you find out that the world didn't end, you can proceed to the next oldest month, and so on. Before too long, proceeding at your own pace, you'll have completely eliminated the need for such a file.

You'll find that you use your contact manager or database more often, find things more readily, and feel more confident. You've come a long way, baby. You're ready to apply techniques that work for your individual learning styles.

Paper Clutter and Filing Systems

Often organizational issues are not organizational at all.
People are not motivated, not attached to the outcome.
Kinesthetic or visual people are using the wrong system.
Trying to improve methods not in line with their values
won't work. You waste all your energy trying to be
disciplined enough to make other systems work for you and
then you have no energy to spend on what really matters.

—Lynn Cutts Personal Coach,
www.manageyourmuse.com

Paper Clutter

Key Concepts

1. Date all files.

2. Reduce decision-making.

3. Nest projects so you can find things quickly.

4. **Always** say "HI"—"How Important Is It?"

Paper clutter is the number one problem for most offices, according to statistics provided by the National Association of Professional Organizers and my own interviews.

▶ Forty-five new sheets of paper are generated each day for each office worker.

▶ An average of 19 copies are made of each original.

▶ Almost two trillion pieces of paper are generated yearly in American offices.

▶ Executives spend up to six weeks each year searching for misplaced, misfiled, or mislabeled paperwork.

▶ Record keeping constitutes more than 90 percent of all office activity. (North Carolina's *Brunswick Beacon*)

Personal Perspectives

A secretary in a medical clinic put it like this: "Working so many hours each day, and leaving just as security was locking up meant I didn't have enough time at my desk to do paper work. I was in a clinic setting most of the time, and could only leave when we were done. There was so much to be done, by the time I had a day off from clinic, I felt overwhelmed."

An office manager put it succinctly, "I think some people just save too much of old and not required stuff."

Ed Udelle, Chicago Operations Manager of 1-800-GOT-JUNK (*www.1800gotjunk.com*) said, "My job requires a lot of time to review items prior to filing. So paper ends up spread out across my desk, subject to review before filing. Other tasks require me to be out in the field, tapping available hours to get organized. Organization is handled on a priority basis where I sometimes catch up, only to later be inundated with more paper."

A Non-filing System Is More Important Than a Filing System

Experience continues to show that 30-40 percent of all recorded information can be immediately deleted from electronic systems or paper systems, because 30-40 percent of all recorded information in the average organization is unnecessary duplicate copies of records that are maintained elsewhere in the organization. (*Office Systems* March 1997, Dr. Mark Langemo CRM)

Before you create a great filing system, create a great **non-filing system.** Keeping this river of information that flows into our offices from flooding our desks is more important than anything else we can do.

Mail

"At one office mailroom in the Seattle area, a six-week study showed that the mailroom staff was spending 25 percent of its time sorting Standard Class (formerly Third Class) advertising mail.

"At the Minneapolis office of a major financial services corporation, they receive more than **40,000 pieces** of advertising mail every month, and discard almost 88 percent of that mail. They dispose of more than **68 tons** of unwanted mail every year. The company estimates that it costs them more than **$75,000 a year** to deal with this unwanted mail."

(Source, *The Business Junk Mail Reduction Project.*)

Rules That Stop Mail Clutter for All Types of Learners

Rule #1: Mail doesn't belong in an in-box. Make a "mail-box."

Rule #2: Make an appointment daily to deal with mail.

Rule #3: Visually scan documents and automatically eliminate the useless.

Rule #4: Whenever possible, make an entry in your contact manager.

Rule #5: Unless you have an important reason to have a paper backup, don't.

Here is a step-by-step example of how to deal with a letter from a customer or supplier:

Step #1: Don't put it in your in-box. Have a separate "mail-box." Compartmentalizing tasks makes it easier to do them in blocks of time.

Step #2: At the "mail appointment" time, open it.

Step #3:   Learn to scan (visually, not with your computer). While junk
            is getting harder to identify by the envelope, some mail can be
            eliminated immediately upon opening. As soon as you open an
            envelope, you should be able to tell by the first paragraph if it:

            1.   Doesn't apply to your business.

            2.   Is from someone trying to sell you something you
                 don't need or want.

            3.   Is not from a customer, won't make you money or
                 help your business operate better.

            If it fits those criteria, jump to Rule #5—trash it.

Step #4:   If it is from a customer or supplier, before you file it, deter-
            mine its relevancy. If the contents can be summarized in a
            paragraph or two, type it into your database under the
            customer's/supplier's name or company. Whether you are us-
            ing *Act!*, Outlook, Access, or a personalized database pro-
            gram, the format should be something like this:

            Customers (The Group)
                 Customer name or company
                      In the "Notes" section, write the date "Received letter"

Leave an Abbreviation Trail to Help Those Who Follow You

A uniform set of action abbreviations will save time and confusion.
Use the first letter of common actions, and just enough letters to make
what you've done clear, understandable, and easily read by others. I man-
aged credit departments for Citibank and a hospital. We used the same
set of abbreviations, department-wide. If I died, the next drone could
follow-up easily. "TR"—Telephoned Residence. "TB"—Telephoned Business. "RL"—Received Letter. "RTL"—Responded To Letter. "WNL"—
Wrote New Letter. "FU"—(No, not what you think) on mm/dd/yy for Follow
Up on a certain date.

Standardize the date format for **your** business. Much of the world
uses a different system. If your business deals mainly with international
clients, you may need to retrain your American employees to switch. A
travel agent told me that the different formats cause confusion—a nine-
letter word for clutter.

Done and Done

Type the subject of the letter. For example: "Orders are late." Use as few words as possible to identify the situation. Type the important information, assign a follow-up action and date. You are done with that letter.

Rule #5:   When you've entered the important information, throw away/ shred the letter. Unless you need the paper file for a CYA situation, or if you are a lawyer, accountant, or financial advisor, don't keep it.

Will this take longer than filing the letter? A little. Will it save time later? Absolutely. Not only have you dealt with the piece of paper (and the human being who wrote it), but you decided on the next action. Since it is in your computer, and has been assigned a follow-up date, you won't forget it. Had you filed it in your filing cabinet, you'd have to take more steps to follow up later.

What If It Requires Further Action?

Some things, like invitations, can't be resolved on the first pass. We all get mail that can't be decided upon right away. Mark Farley once told me, "On my desk, right now, are an invitation to a party and one to a wedding. They tend to stay on my desk because I don't know what to do with them. There is no business file to put them in because they aren't business related."

Make the association that works best for you with a visualization and put the personal items in a personal hanging file. Invitations need to go into a date file, which you check every day. The dates also need to be put into your calendar. Schedule the date you need to take action in your contact manager, set an alarm, and get the paper off your desk. You don't need it anymore.

Apply the same principles as above. The difference is you have to make entries for "The Task" (Conference or Speaking Engagements), besides the Company. Why? Because our minds file information in categories. While you might remember that "Reynolds Corp." asked you to speak at their annual convention, you are more likely to remember that you are supposed to speak somewhere someday.

Make a second entry.

> Speaking Engagement (or Conferences)
> Note: See Reynolds Corp.

Under this heading, make as many entries as necessary. Keep the information under the company entry. Do not duplicate it here. When you have two files with information, one will invariably be out-of-date.

Mailing Lists

When I was on the *Dr. Laura Show*, we got a call from a woman who was distraught about all the mail she received. I said, "You could remove yourself from mailing lists, but the fastest, most practical solution is to pitch catalogs, solicitations, and other irrelevant information immediately." Dr. Laura agreed and does the same thing herself. Sometimes the simple solutions are the best solutions.

Businesses can remove their names from mailing lists through *http://dnr.metrokc.gov/swd/nwpc/bizjunkmail.htm*. Individuals and home businesses can go to the Direct Marketing Association's site, *www.thedma.org/consumers/offmailinglist.html*. Remember, though, every time you ask for a catalog or use your credit card, you may be "requesting" new junk mail.

It takes about a year to get off the lists. These companies purge their lists in: January, April, July, and October. One businesswoman told me that after two years, she gets about an inch of mail daily, down from four inches. Out of spite, she returns junk mail in the postage-reply envelopes if possible.

Catalog Clutter

According to the US Postal Service more than 14 billion catalogs and were delivered to US offices and households in 1998. Americans received approximately 104 catalogs and 76 magazines per address. (Source: "USPS 1998 Report." Cited in *Office PRO,* Sept. 99.)

Do you mostly use one supplier? Can you order online? Then you don't need monthly catalogs from three others. Time wasted to save 30 cents on a case of file folders isn't worth time spent comparing them. Save a tree. Save time.

I consulted with a company whose purchasing agent got 10 office supply catalogs monthly. He said he saved the company money by comparison shopping. In reality, he compared the free offers of junk gifts suppliers offered. He kept the trinkets. We cut him off. The company got off the mailing lists. We discovered that he redirected the catalogs to his home, so he could supply his junk-habit, but the company saved several hours of his time monthly.

Corporations

Appoint a non-cluttering employee as a mail sorter. Besides sorting by addressee, someone could be given clear guidelines on what is junk and keep it out of your cluttering employees' hands in the first place.

The recipients would have to tell the sorter in advance if he or she gets catalogs that just **have** to be delivered.

Self-employed

Separate business from personal mail. Have your business accounts addressed to "Global Mega Business," or whatever you call your entity. There are exceptions, for instance, many home businesspeople don't have a business telephone number, so the phone bill comes in their name. If part of your phone bill is personal and part business, put the bill in the business pile and deal with the financial split later. Any accounting program can split the payment into categories for tax purposes.

Declare a small desk as the mailing center. Have a recycle/trash bin next to it. If your area doesn't recycle yet, don't obsess about what to do with stuff. If you really drive to the recycling center regularly, save it in a recycling bin. If not, it is clutter. Trash it. Absolve yourself temporarily from guilt. You won't destroy the planet if you don't recycle until you get your cluttering habits turned around. Your office should not look like a landfill in progress because of papers you are "going to" recycle.

Phone Message Clutter

If you are an auditory person, use the phone more than e-mail or letters. ADD people also generally do better talking on the phone than by writing. I like the real touch of talking to people and have ways to keep from wasting their time or mine. I don't use a clock. I use my intuition. You can sense when it's time to stop speaking. Polite ways of getting off the phone are: "Well, I'm glad we've taken care of that." "Is there anything else I can do for you?" "I'm going to research your questions right now." Avoid, "So what's the point?"

Most successful businesspeople return calls in bunches, at a pre-set time of day. Having a secretary certainly helps. For those of us who don't, a voicemail system works. Making calls shortly before lunch shortens them. Making them at the end of the day, when everyone wants to go home makes even the most loquacious person less verbose.

Some businesses require that we answer the phone and help customers right away. Software "customer service" companies and Internet providers seem to be immune from this disorder, though.

I **strongly dislike** phone message pads for small businesses. They just create one more piece of paper to lose. In a corporation, you may be stuck with them. What works best, and creates the least clutter are two things. Always have your contact manager open. Enter the customer's messages right away. Then you don't need a paper backup. You can also copy and paste the info into a document to save time if you have to reply.

The other method is to have a simple 8 1/2 × 11 spiral notebook by the phone. **Buy one with an easy-to-spot, outlandish cover.** Date the top of the page and write messages on the page. You could get fancy and put colored tabs for each week, but I haven't found that worthwhile. Everything is in date order and in one place.

Filing Systems That Work for Clutterers of All Types

Key Concepts

1. Date all files.

2. Reduce decision-making.

Only about 20 percent of the papers you file are referred to again. Yet, an average of 60 percent of each person's time is now spent processing documents. (*Data Smog*, derived from Patrick Ames, *Beyond Paper*).

Make your filing system work like your brain, based on your learning style. There is no one perfect system.

The only "have to" is to write the date filed (month/date/year, or simply month/year, as you choose) in the upper right hand corner of every file. Why? Once you've learned to trust your decisions, you'll actually enjoy purging your filing cabinet. This makes it easier. "Every file older than X date goes," will reduce decision-making. The fewer decisions we have to make, the easier it is to stay decluttered.

Computer-based Solutions

Myth 1: A scanner will solve all my filing problems.

I have a paper document from a potential supplier named Appleton about a new telephone system. I take about three minutes to place it on the scanner, scan it, and then file it on my hard drive. Oops, make that six minutes because the OCR missed a few words. Since hard drives crash, and I'm not very good at backing up, I'd better file this paper just to be safe. That takes another two minutes. Total time elapsed: eight minutes. Likelihood this will be important: 20 percent.

Solution

Before filing or scanning anything, say HI. Is this new information, or merely a follow-up to something else? A typical business letter contains about 30 percent fluff. From the letterhead to the inside address, there's nothing useful.

If the letter or fax is merely an acknowledgment of your last fax or letter, then a quick note in your contact manager will suffice.

If it contains new, useful information, can it be summarized and computerized, or do you need the paper as a CYA document? Some businesses are more CYA-prone than others, so use good judgment. A little paranoia can be a good thing.

Finding a system that balances clutter-proofing your business with your personal style is a trial and error process. If you try to apply a rigid system that makes you feel uncomfortable, it will fail. Finding balance is the goal.

If the entire document is worth keeping, scan it. File it under a filing system that makes it easy to retrieve.

Myth 2: If I keep everything in my computer, I can find it.

Having everything on your computer or PDA is no guarantee you'll be able to find it easily. Instead of doing a "Find" search for "Appleton" every time you need his documents, learn to file intelligently. **Do not put everything into "My Documents."** For one thing, it's the first place viruses and worms look. For another, this directory gets cluttered when you use it for everything. A proper filing system saves you from wading through dozens of documents to find the one you want.

Solution

Keep it simple, but not too simple. The problem with taking a Zen minimalist approach to filing (computer or paper) is that we are **not** Zen masters. Our minds are more like a fragmented computer file. Have you ever defragged your files? You should at least once a week. Otherwise, you won't be able to find anything.

Our minds don't file information sequentially, by priority, or alphabetically. We mentally file by association.

Directory Structure

Telephone System Bidders
    Requirements Info Sent to all Bidders
        Appleton
            Notes and letters from me
                Pricing
                    Special Features
            Notes and letters from Appleton
                Pricing
                    Special Features
        Bidder 2
            Notes and letters from me
                Pricing
                    Special Features
            Notes and letters from Bidder 2
                Pricing
                    Special Features
        Bidder 3
            Notes and letters from me
                Pricing
                    Special Features
            Notes and letters from Bidder 3
                Pricing
                    Special Features
    Discussions Meeting Notes
        First Meeting
            (You could make folders by ideas or people presenting them.)
        Second Meeting
    Final Report Due Before 9/15/03

A nested hierarchal filing system like this helps you quickly find pertinent information. You can collapse the directory to show only the big picture or expand it to find a specific supplier.

Redundant Filing on Your Computer

Redundant filing helps on your computer, just as in paper filing. Use the same categories to trigger your memory in your contact manager or database as you do with paper filing.

The telephone project could get you a promotion. Make a directory:

> Promotion
> > See Telephone Files

Paper-Based Filing Systems

Myth 3: There is only one way to file papers.

Even if your company demands that you adhere to their vision of filing, there is still hope. You may still be able to place dummy files that jog your memory and help you find files in their system. It takes a little more space in your filing cabinet, but you'll have more space because you declutter on a regular basis.

Solution

You already know to say HI before filing anything. If you've decided you really need to file a document, make sure you and your coworkers can find it later.

There's nothing more aggravating when you are sick, after you've taken some wonder medicine to knock you out and snuggled in for a day's rest, then getting a call from a boss or co-worker because she can't find important files.

You are groggy and can't visualize the office. You don't want to waste valuable energy, better spent on fighting microbes, trying to remember where the file on someone named Appleton is. All you want to do is sleep. Resentment builds up. You get snappish. The drugs have lowered your natural inhibitions and you say what you really think about your job and boss. You are fired and lose your health benefits. You have to go to a public clinic. You end up dead or crippled for life. All this could have been avoided if you'd used a redundant filing system.

Tailor this, or any, system to your learning style.

Any filing system needs to be adapted to your own best method of learning and remembering. A combination of filing systems is presented in this redundant filing system. Use the parts that will work for you. If the redundant aspect doesn't work for you (but please try it, you might be pleasantly surprised), use the different types of filing styles in a project-oriented system, and skip the redundant step. If you can get by with plain vanilla alphabetical filing, and just adding a few memory joggers, then you are well along the road to being organized. As our confidence in our abilities improves, most of us can eliminate the redundancies.

Whether you are making a backup for a scanned document or simply filing something in a paper file, apply the first criteria, HI—"How important is it?"

Visualization is the key.

Strive for Dominance

When you have the scene firmly in your mind, what sense seems to be dominant? Your emotions? Colors of the surroundings? Roaring of the crowd? Your boss's or spouse's voice? The feeling of being physically touched by your spouse, boss, teammates? That dominant emotion is the key to helping you remember. If the dominant feeling conflicts with your answers on the questionnaire, go with your feelings now. Sometimes we are too logical when taking a test. Our feelings don't lie. You are probably a combination of two learning types and one might fit better with using a filing system. Try both for awhile and see which one works. You'll know pretty quickly. Don't forget the power of humor! Whatever you can do to make a project humorous will make it stick with you. You could visualize the telephone project as a skit about someone getting lost in voice mail hell, or a Lucille Ball-type episode of a harried old-fashioned telephone operator.

Don't Just File It and Forget It

Reviewing what you did after you've done it has proven to dramatically improve retention. Remember those nerds in school who always had the right answers? If you had asked them what they did that was different than you, they would have said they took good notes and reviewed them before the day was over. The short amount of time you'll spend reviewing where you just filed things will pay big rewards in finding them later.

Memory by Association

Make a mental "hanger" to prod your memory to put the project in its right place. Memory experts (you know, those smart alecks who can recite everyone's name in a crowd of a hundred) tell us that one secret is to associate a person's name with something else. "Mike Nelson" might be too common to remember, but if you associate the name with the old *Seahunt* TV series and visualize me in full scuba gear, you'll pick me out of a lineup. "Janis Wilson" is common, but if you visualize her on a January calendar as a sun-face willing to work, you won't forget her name. Personalize the hanger using your dominant learning type.

Visual: "I see the light filing"

A quick visualization will imprint a file's location in your memory quicker and better than anything else. You don't have to get cross-legged and chant in order to visualize. Visualization is merely creating a mental image of what you want to remember. You then associate the image with pegs that jog your particular type of memory: sounds, colors, emotions, funny images, whatever helps you to remember. You are creating what psychologists call "attachment." Attachment means that we make things personal.

Another reason for visualization is that it makes work more fun. The project may be boring, you may resent it, but at least you can get a giggle from it when you have to work on it. Making dreary work fun will help you organize.

We are more likely to sabotage ourselves and misfile things when we aren't happy. While we can't all have dream jobs and still feed our families, we can make what we do less of a chore. It will pay off in the long run in being organized.

First, let's double-check the test you took on learning styles. Think of any strongly positive event that has been deeply imbedded in your consciousness. Examples are: the time you were praised by your boss for doing something spectacular, the day your spouse proposed, or the time you won a high school football game. Take some time to relieve this without distractions.

Marita Adair is a visual, creative person. Her secret to being able to find anything later is to **see** it. She uses four-legged wire shelves, to put the scanner above her printer, under-shelf wire baskets, plastic see-through crates as book dividers on her shelves and clear literature containers. "I can organize my clutter better if I can see it. I mark on my daily calendar to put away 12 things. I often accomplish a lot more, particularly if I grab items as I pass by them rather than leaving them out of place day after day."

Visual people should use transparent "Action" files on their desks while working on a project, then transfer them to transparent filing crates as it loses its immediacy. Once it goes into the metal monster filing cabinet, it is like declaring them dead and buried.

Use see-through filing systems whenever possible. Use flowcharts (both visual and logical tools) to map activities. Use charts on the wall to keep track of where you are in your task list. Map the filing system in the file cabinets you use. Keep the map where we can see it. That way we can "see our way through."

Kinesthetic: "Touchy-feely filing"

Kinesthetic people can keep a file folder filled with sticky notes with the names of each file that they can move around as they use them. Make a file folder (a legal size is best for you) that you can access readily. Keep it on your desk instead of the files themselves. Write the names of the real file folders on sticky notes. This frees you to put the files in a real file drawer and not feel like you have "lost touch" with them. When you need a file, go to your sticky note folder. As the project moves forward, you can move the notes into different stages like "waiting on a call from Appleton," "submitted bid to Appleton," "pending installation," etc.

Auditory: "I can hear you knocking."

Auditory people can associate a sound with the file. Since reading has a strong auditory component for many of us, go ahead and say it out loud. You are already "saying" it in your mind. This reinforces it. For instance, when you begin this telephone project, say out loud, "Telephone Systems." Then visualize a phone ringing. Imbed that sound into your mind. Pull in a little association, and visualize an apple tree with a ringing phone for Appleton. Hear the phone ring again. You could imagine an old-fashioned page-boy walking through the office saying, "Phone message for Mr. Appleton. Phone message for Mr. Appleton." Now you have the entire project and the individual characters in the plot impressed on your auditory senses. If you've talked to any of the people involved, recall the sound of their voices as you create files for them. Whenever someone sounds like somebody you already know or a TV or radio voice, associate their name with the name of the person they sound like.

Logical Learners Can Eliminate the Next Step.

Logical learners won't need the redundant filing system. If they've set the files up in a logical manner, they will feel comfortable that they can find them.

Emotional: "I feel filing"

Emotional learners will add their own emotional reactions to the previous mental visualizations above to make the project and people important to them. I know it's hard to get emotional about a telephone system, but you don't have to get all logical about it. In fact, you probably should drop all pretenses to being logical right now. You could visualize a telephone call where you got some really good news. Hear the voice on the other end, but in a different way than the auditory learners. Hear the emotions in the other person's voice and feel the emotions in yours. Then add in the main players in the project or names of the folders in a conversation with the person giving you the news. Hear Appleton excitedly telling you about his proposal.

How Should I File?

You decide a letter or fax from Appleton is important enough to file. You make a folder. Now the decision-making process begins. This is when a clutterer starts sweating. Should you file it under "A" for Appleton, (alphabetical), "To Do RIGHT AWAY!" (priority), or "T" for "Telephone Systems," which is what the deal is all about (project). Should you file it under "P" for "pointless," since this deal isn't going anywhere anyway (sure method to unemployment system)?

A filing system is supposed to make life easier for you. **Never forget that. How do you remember best?**

Project System

Create a hanging file for "Telephone Systems." Add a file folder for "Appleton." Avoid making one labeled "Pointless."

This is logical and called "The Project System." It works well with projects that have different people associated with them. Putting the players under "Telephone Systems" is quite logical. The best explanation of this (and much, much more) is in a book, *Take Back Your Time* (St. Martin's Griffin, 1999) by Jan Jasper. Jan has a very good understanding about what works for clutterers as well as non-clutterers. She is a productivity and time-management consultant in New York City and highly recommended. Her newsletter is very much worth getting to help keep on track.

The Redundancy System

Before you dismiss this unorthodox filing system, try it. Organized people don't understand it. Clutterers do. The already organized thought it was too complicated. Clutterers think it works for the way they think. I've tried it myself and in some offices infested with clutterers for about a year. It can work when traditional systems alone fail. It doesn't eliminate traditional systems. It enhances them. Combine it with color-coding, project filing, or any other method you use.

Use the "Project System" above, but add something to help you remember. We are seldom logical. We remember people or companies better than we remember projects. We need to make a hanging file for "Appleton." But we can't file anything there. Someone else who doesn't know Appleton won't be able to find it. She was told by the boss to root through your files and get all the quotes about the telephone system project. So you have to cover yourself on two levels.

Within the hanging file for Appleton, put half a file folder with the heading "See Telephone Systems." To eliminate the possibility of filing something in the "referral file" cut the folder in half. You won't be able to file anything by mistake there because there's only half a folder. But it will help you remember where it should go. Do the same thing for all the bidders. If doing this project right might get you a promotion, add a second hanging file, "Promotion."

Color Coding

Color-coding works well for most people, especially visual learners. Make the project files all the same color. Unfortunately, there are only so many colors and way too many projects. To choose a color, use visualization. Think about the project with your eyes closed and see what color comes to you.

What does red look like? What does it sound like?

Use emotions, sounds, logic, sights—whatever works for you to determine the "right" color. If you think of the red hotline in the President's office, red wins. If you visualize people yelling at each other, use yellow. If you visualize someone talking until they are blue in the face, go for blue. There is no one way to choose a color. Clutterers agonize over the most trivial things. We are likely to waste 20 minutes picking the "right" color for a project file, when two minutes would have been plenty.

Don't use a rainbow when one color will do.

Choosing a second color for the individual bidders might help you keep them clear. But be careful, **too much "organization" is complication.** Try it to see if it helps before you get married to such a system. It could lead to confusion with future projects. Using small colored dots rather than colored folders is better. Tape them to the folder, since they fall off when you use the files repeatedly. Appleton screams for red (a ripe apple). The possibility that he and the project may have the same color isn't important. This occasionally happens.

Do not use colored plastic tabs for the hanging folders. They may add an artistic flair, but it is nearly impossible to read the labels.

Planning Ahead

Don't stop with just choosing a cute color. Make a color key map and tape it to the front of the filing cabinet, and write a note named "color code" in your contact manager. This makes it easier for you and everyone else to find files. A little planning ahead will keep them from calling you at home when you are sick. That may save your job. In Outlook, you can adjust the colors for the fonts of different activities.

Use fifth-cut file folders. Before you start filing, arrange them according to the position of the cut. Their drawback is that they don't offer much space to write. With fifth cut folders, there is mathematically less of a chance one file will be behind another. The idea is to be able to see the heading of each folder. Two folders with their heading directly behind each other might as well not be there. Your filing system should look like this (see page 124):

Telephone System Bidders (Red hanging folder) [6/2/03]
    Preliminary info all bidders (1st cut)
        Appleton (2nd cut red or green dot for apples) [6/2/03]
           Bidder 2 (3rd cut) [8/03]

Telephone System Project

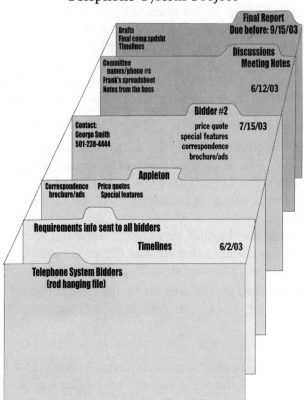

Bidder 3 (4th cut) [7/15/03]

Discussions, Meeting Notes (5th cut) [6/2/03]

Final Report (1st cut again) Due BEFORE 9/15/03

For the illogical among us, add a redundant file.

Appleton

See Telephone System Bidders

Promotion

See Telephone System Bidders

More Filing Myths

Myth 4: I can find it. If I make it too easy for others, I will lose my importance.

We've all heard stories about companies that begged the retired secretary or office assistant to come back to work because no one could find anything. Some people purposely create complicated, secretive filing systems to increase their own value to their employer.

Sometimes they know their jobs so well that their system isn't created out of fear, but because of their intimate knowledge. Sometimes a cluttered filing system is caused by a cluttered mind. Regardless of the reason, the results are the same: an incomprehensible system to anyone else.

Here is an example given me by an employee of a nonprofit historical foundation. It could be representative of any organization that puts on festivals or annual entertainment events. Career coaches and professional organizers unanimously agree that nonprofits tend to be the most disorganized type of business.

Among other activities, the organization put on an annual event based on Charles Dickens characters. The person in charge of filing knew the Dickens characters, so she filed information by character. But, since she wanted to insure her value and her job, she took it a step farther. The filing system worked but only as long as she did. Due to her superior knowledge, she could justify it.

A logical filing system would have been something like:

    Dickens Festival
        Characters
            Queen Victoria
            Mr. Bumble
            Tiny Tim
            Etc.
        Talent
            Performer 1
            Performer 2
        Suppliers
            Banners
            Refreshments
            Etc.

Instead, she did this:

    Victoria, Queen
    Tim, Tiny
    Mr., Bumble

Mondo (Name of Talent)

Bill Smith (Company Owner's Name of Banner Supplier)

Gonzalez, Hank (Salesman for Coca Cola Supplier)

Withers, Ann (name of person who played Queen Victoria)

There was no hierarchy. She obfuscated the information by making the first word one less likely to be someone's first thought. Most of us think of "Queen Victoria" and "Tiny Tim." We tend to ignore Mr., Ms., Mrs., and think of a person's name, for example, "Bumble." A newcomer would be unlikely to know that Mondo was the contact for The Texas Magician's Union. If we didn't know that Bill Smith was the owner of Acme Graphics, the banner supplier, or that Hank (whose first name really was Enrique) Gonzalez was the salesman for Coca Cola, we'd never know where to look.

This all came to a head when she left of her own accord and a new person took over. It took months to unravel the mess.

Solution

This is a difficult situation. If only one person is doing this, she may need reassurance. If more than one person has adopted this, or other paranoia-induced job protection measures, you have a bigger problem. It might call for a serious evaluation of your company's way of treating your employees. If your company is operating in a fear mode that causes people to protect themselves, it's going to take more than changing filing systems to make things right.

If only one person created this maze, she will look at any help as outside interference and just a way to get rid of her.

It is a good idea to have another employee (preferably a supervisor) occasionally look in employees' files to see if they make sense. This has to be done company-wide, with tact. If you do it with one employee, she will feel persecuted. A persecuted employee is a dangerous employee.

Send a company-wide memo that, in the interests of cross-training, (efficiency or whatever buzzword you choose) someone will evaluate the filing system of all employees. (Obviously, those who have sensitive documents have to be evaluated by someone with the proper clearance).

When you find little rock-pools of stagnant filing systems, have someone with some compassion and common sense prepare a recommendation based on the principles in this chapter.

You'll get howls of dismay from these creative filers. They will say that they won't be able to find anything if you mess with their files. They'll remind you that they were filing this way long before you came to the company. (The unspoken part of that is, "And I'll be doing it long after you are gone.")

Creative filers make redundant files to help themselves, but only themselves. Give people latitude to make redundant files that help them do their jobs, but don't let them create minefields that could blow up your business.

Myth 5: Action files will keep me on track.

These can be useful, but they are more often overused. It's okay to have a portable file container on your desk with things you really, really need to work on today, but the chances for abuse are great. Look at it this way: if you are trying to lose weight, you might take an appetite suppressant for a few days. But, if you keep them around and gobble one every time you feel a little hungry, you will become addicted. The same goes for "action" files. You need to change your habits so that these helpers don't become a way of life.

Ongoing projects shouldn't be kept in action files when there's no action occuring. Re-file them when you complete an action. Every day there's a new set of things that cry out for action. If nothing ever moves out of there, you can't take any action because "in-action" files have taken over your desk.

Solution

Allow yourself three action files. If something comes up during the day that you need to work on, get the file from the filing cabinet. If you need to make a new file, replace something from your so-called "action" area with the new one, or file it away. Make it a habit to stop an hour before you leave the office and finish up the files on your desk. Then file them where they belong. If you need them tomorrow, you will know right where they are.

Make a set of "Pending" files you can keep nearby (so they won't feel left out) in a rollaway hanging file basket. When we get them off the desk, into a pending folder, we can give all our attention to the project at hand. Mark Farley, President of Inter-Networks, (*www.teach-english-mexico.com*) operates an international business from his home, placing teachers in positions in Mexico. "I use both types of files. Teachers about to be placed in a position go into a hanging file on the desk in a see-through file. When they are placed, they go into a regular file. I file by name. Each teacher has name or and each of my sales reps have a name."

This Is Only the Start

You will find new tools and techniques based on your individual style. Use them. What have you got to lose? Only your clutter. When you discover something that works for you, you feel creative. The suggestions here will open your mind that has been stuck in thinking there is only one way to do things. There are many paths to the same destination. Some may take the scenic route, and if that's what works for you, meander along. No matter how odd your style may seem to an organized person, if it works for you, **and** you can leave a trail of breadcrumbs for them to follow, you'll get to Grandma's cottage just the same. It will be more fun because your reward will be milk and cookies instead of a Big Bad Wolf of disorganization.

Home Offices

Don't mix personal and business.
This includes calls, catalogs, mail, etc.
Try not to bring business home.
If you overlap that's really messy.
That's cluttering your mind. It's also the most frequent
mistake people who work at home make.

—Karen Griggs, MFT, Marriage Family Counselor,
Burbank, Calif.

Key Concepts

1. Home and office are two words. Keep the rooms that way.

2. Being close to your kids doesn't mean having them in the office.

3. Clutter is anything, physical or mental, that doesn't relate to the task at hand.

4. Clutterers need more stuff on their desks and in our offices than non-clutterers to feel comfortable.

5. Make your schedule fit your personal style, but make it.

Clutter Is the Culprit

> "There is an entirely different dynamic of clutter in home-based businesses."
> —Linda Durham, Professional Organizer,
> *www.organizingmatters.com*

Clutter is a thief. It steals your time. It defeats you. These specific suggestions are based on my having operated successful home businesses and interviews with several home-based business owners.

Cluttering runs rampant when we work at home. We have to deal with two devils at once—home and office clutter. When we were cube-dwellers or glass office captives, at least we could deal with them separately. Home-office workers overwhelmingly said their cluttering worsened when they moved their work to their home.

Who Stole My Time?

Besides the millions of people who run businesses from home, 20 million Americans work from home at least once a week, according to the *Wall Street Journal*. Although this group consists mostly of managerial and sales workers, most teachers have "homework" too. The ideas here will apply to anyone who works at home, for any length of time.

Working from home gives us more time—36 hours a year of not being stuck in traffic (Texas Transportation Institute) and 47.6 minutes a day (coming and going, according to the latest U.S. Census data). If you live in Los Angeles, you get a bonus of seven days a year of not being stuck in traffic that doesn't move. Put it all together and you save about six weeks of commuting time. Are you getting six weeks more work done?

One reason people start home-based businesses is that their corporate and personal goals clash. How can you spend more time with your family, develop a meaningful relationship, or just have a social life if you are on the road four days out of five? How can you help with raising your kids if you work 80 or more hours a week?

Sometimes, we just want the "freedom" that working for ourselves promises. Many owners of home-based businesses have found that to be an empty promise. They routinely say, "I wanted to work part-time. I just didn't know it would be the largest part of my life."

We are working more hours and making less money. What's wrong?

> "First you have to learn to prioritize. That is number one.
> Keep coming back to the number one priority. Maybe you
> only get that one thing done some days."
> —Karen, office manager for home-based dental office

We often work 80 hours a week and wonder where our time went. Just like office workers, we should reexamine our priorities. The next step is making a schedule. Wait a minute—that's what you hated about working for someone else, that you had to adhere to a schedule. It wasn't the schedule; it was that it was someone else's schedule you resented.

Make time for what's really important.

If you left the corporate world to have more time with your family, make them a priority. Put them down as an appointment. Want to have dinner together? Make it an appointment. Want to have time to date or socialize with your friends? Make an appointment.

There will always be one more project to do, one more call to make or letter to write. Fear that you are losing money by not doing them is always breathing down your neck.

Doing some of those things tomorrow won't make a whit of difference in the long run. Real projects with real deadlines are one thing. Whirling around without direction is another.

When we are self-employed, we assign equal importance to everything. (Which is similar to why some ADD people have a hard time focusing). We lose sight of the Big Picture. Remember, you are in charge. Before you run off willy-nilly, starting projects and soliciting business, ask yourself, as CEO, how important is this, really? Say "HI" to what you doing, as well as your papers.

It's easy to fall into the trap of thinking we are "small" businesspeople. We aren't. We are niche businesspeople. We provide service or customer care that the bigger corporations don't. We have product knowledge that they don't. Instead of some clerk who juggles a dozen product lines, or just takes orders, we are on the front lines. **We are the product.** Software that processes orders faster won't make as much difference as getting ourselves organized.

Remember Why You Started Your Business?

1. To have more time with family or to have a social life.

2. To have more freedom.

3. To do something that was challenging and stimulating.

4. To make more money.

Are these unfulfilled promises? We've usually reversed our priorities. Money should be the last priority, because if we take care of the first three, the money will be there.

If our goals center around having more time with our family, how can we achieve that if we spend more time at work? We've eliminated the commute, but have we gained anything if we spend more time in front of the computer or on the phone?

Remember the Big Picture

Make a calendar based on what you want to achieve, not what you think you need to do. Take care of the Big Picture first and the little things will work out.

TIME USAGE CHART

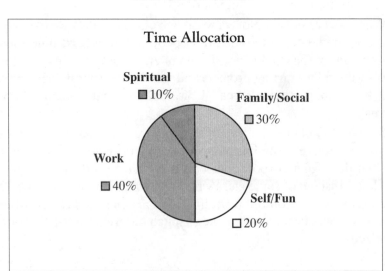

Keep this chart in plain view at all times. Now, keep a record of the time you actually spend during your typical days for two weeks. You'll be amazed at where you time really goes. Likely, relatively unimportant tasks are stealing your time because they are urgent, but not critical. Read Stephen Covey's *The 7 Habits Of Highly Effective People* (Simon & Schuster, 1990) again. We have the power to plan our day around what is really important to us, not let our day be planned by the urgent, but really secondary, events. We just need to learn how to use it.

Your Office Isn't a Day Care Center—Or Maybe It Is

I hear you thinking, "It's my office and I want to be close to my kids." Unless you have a young child you need to watch, love your kids more by giving them their own space. Mothers have told me that generally, children should be 6 years or older to be in another room without your keeping an eye on them. Whether having them do their drawings and school work next to you will work or not depends on the kid. If your child it is constantly distracting you from your work, see if you can set up a separate space as her own "office."

Everything in this book is about individuals, so do what works for you. Susan is a home-based worker and she says, "My son is unobtrusive and can work at the same desk as I do. He is home-schooled and does his lessons next to me. He understands my needs for work and actually raises his hand when he needs to ask me a question."

I have been asked to help many people with home offices and commonly see kid's toys, clothes, or even dishes cluttering up the area. One woman I worked with had a nice computer desk and a great ergonomic chair but couldn't use it, because it held a laundry basket, two Tonka trucks, and a pile of clothes that covered the file folders on the bottom of the chair. There was so much child debris around that her fax machine was stuffed over on the kitchen counter.

We'll talk about how we got her chair back in a little while. Right now, we are concentrating on the kid challenge.

Another woman had a child's desk next to hers, which was cluttered with crayons, paints, and cut-out animals her daughter was working on. Here's what she told me.

"I'm a single mom and I've worked at home as a technical writer for five years. I really like not commuting, or being around people I don't like. At first, I was wildly successful, with more jobs than I could handle. I took on every one because I was afraid there might not be anymore. To complete them, I had to work 14 hours a day. This didn't seem to fit into my life-plan of having more time with my daughter, Samantha, so I 'solved' the problem by putting her desk next to mine, so we could be close. At first, it worked well, and I appreciated the time we had together. But, when I have a deadline to meet, her frequent interruptions get on my nerves. 'Mommy, look at the frog I just drew.' That's nice, dear, I would say, barely glancing at the picture. She could sense I wasn't really paying attention, so she'd follow up with, 'Why are frogs green? What's the difference between a frog and a toad?' I realized that giving her half my attention wasn't going to save any time. When I moved her table into her room, she got angry. 'You don't love me anymore! You're sending me to the dungeon.' What can I do?"

Boundaries Make Good Neighbors

By eliminating the boundaries between your kid's lives and yours, you are just encouraging and teaching them to clutter. Your kids may be the **reason** you work, but they are not **part of** the work. Give them their own space. Doing so will teach them boundaries and a sense of organization. It will help them make natural separations with less stress.

Mary had a couple of problems. Behind every good intention, there is a shadow intention. Briefly, our Shadow Self is like a sack of "ought to" we carry around with us. We "ought to" be devoted to our kids. The good intention was to have more time with her daughter. The shadow intention was the fear that she couldn't balance work and home life any better at home than when she worked in the corporate world.

Her solution seemed to be logical. A clutterer priding herself on being logical is like a baseball pitcher priding himself on his batting ability.

Mary's situation was difficult, but not unsolvable. By setting up an "office" in Samantha's room, with places for her crayons, scissors, paper, books, school notebooks, etc., it gave her a sense of her own place. To help her overcome Samantha's initial feelings of rejection, Mary dropped in to several times a day to see how she was doing for the first few weeks. Samantha began to appreciate having her own space and eventually asked Mary to "stop interrupting her work." From the mouths of babes.

What Is Different About Home Clutter?

At home, our personal space flows into our work space. Don't let it. Laundry belongs in the laundry room. Dishes belong in the kitchen. Mail belongs in a designated mail area. None of these things belong on your desk. Almost all of my respondents said their cluttering got worse when they worked at home. Even if you don't have a separate room for an office, there is hope. Mary French was profiled in the *Wall Street Journal* for her philanthropic project of putting a dictionary into the hands of every third-grader in South Carolina (*www.dictionaryproject.org*). She works from a table in her living room. Still, she keeps personal mail and clutter from intruding. She's learned the "sacred space" principle of keeping only things that belong in one place. "I keep only business-related items on the table. I don't have a PDA. I keep everything in my head."

> "Others in the household may also have the tendency to use the workspace designated for the home office and leave items behind on the desk. So not only is there the challenge of keeping the business stuff organized, but you are constantly moving other family stuff out of the way so you can work."
> —Nancy Kruschke, Professional Organizer

Just One More Bit of Research

We often put in long hours, justifying them by, "If I don't do it, it won't get done. If I put just a few more hours (never one or three or some quantifiable limit) into this project, it will pay off 10 (or 100) times."

From dawn to dusk and beyond.

Joe was a stay-at-home stock market trader. The Market opens and closes at the same time every day. But Joe's work was never done.

"During Market hours, I have to react to immediate events. I can't take time for analysis and predictions during Market hours. After the closing bell, I take an hour to unwind, then get back to it. I have to download the day's data, analyze it, read the news released after Market hours and gauge the impact on the next trading day. I take a break to be with my family for dinner, then go back and start crunching numbers and analyzing my trading decisions. Before I know it, it's 1 a.m. My wife is asleep and I am alone. I try to sleep. Sometimes, my mind reels from the work I've done all night. The next day I start it all over."

I hate to say it Joe, but you will never have enough data. I traded for a living and was like you. For every "Aha!" moment you get from divining the secret to stock movements there will be dozens of erroneous conclusions because a) you didn't have all the data or b) you had too much data. Couple that with the mistakes resulting from too little sleep and you'll find yourself on a treadmill to a heart attack.

The same principles apply whether you are building a marketing plan, mapping sales territories, or doing research on the Internet. You can't know everything.

Start Times and Finish Times

Make your home office operate like an office. Start at 9 a.m. (or noon if you are a night owl). Stop at 4 p.m. (6 p.m. for night owls, but don't worry, you get to go back later). Spend some time doing personal or family things. There is one important exception. We have the power to intersperse daily household chores like doing the dishes, washing clothes, vacuuming so that our weekends can be free. We build time for that into our daily schedules.

Where did my day go?

Since we don't have a boss to keep us on track, we fritter away time without realizing it. Our justification is, "At the office, I wasted time in the coffee room. Now I don't do that."

True, but you waste time on the nonessential. Keep a log (just use general times) of **nonessential things you do** for a week or two. Don't keep track of the important stuff you accomplish. Concentrate on wasted time. You have to approach it this way so you'll become acutely aware of what's happening. If it has a lot of notations like: played Freecell, played solitaire, talked to friends...you'll know it's a good list. Everything else I suggest accentuates the positive. But to fight the devil, we have to go to hell.

How We Reclaimed That Chair

The most important concept about home and home office decluttering is to focus on one goal at a time. If the chair in front of our computer is cluttered with extraneous stuff, as in the case earlier in the chapter, our goal is to turn it back into a place to sit down. It isn't to organize all the things on the chair. It is to make the chair useful. The second goal (which is always related to the first) is to make the office into an office.

To reclaim the chair, we dumped everything onto the floor. That made the chair useful for sitting. That was a success. Then we took each group of items on the floor (laundry stuff, kid stuff, etc.) to the room where they should have been. We didn't spend time organizing the closet or the kid's room. That would have delayed us from accomplishing our second, related goal of making the office usable. Too often, we start on a decluttering project and get sidetracked by everything else that needs to be done.

TIME WASTED TABLE				
ACTIVITY	START	END	MINUTES	SOLUTION
Call from friend.	9:15	9:45	30	Advise friends of my working hours.
Personal e-mail.	10:20	10:40	20	Personal is personal. Get a personal e-mail address and check it at a specific time of day.
Decided to wash dishes.	12:00	12:15	15	Household chores are a task. Make an appointment to do them.
Looked for book. Rearranged bookshelf.	1:00	1:45	45	While decluttering is always admirable, there is a specific time to do it. Make an appointment.
Decided I needed a software program. Went to store.	2:30	3:30	60	Unless you need it right now, save errands for later, perhaps combining with family time.
Telephone solicitor.	3:40	3:45	5	Multiply this by five a day and it's a huge waste of time. Get an answering machine.
Bill collectors.	3:50	4:10	20	See first entry. They will wait. Talking to them while you work will disrupt your concentration.
Total Today.			195	
Total Yesterday.			210	
Improvement.			15	YAY!

We do the same thing with the time clutter chart. Our goal is to see how much time we waste. You **know** when you are wasting time. You **know** when a call doesn't relate to the activity you are trying to do.

I've kept the table simple. Don't clutter it up by filling in the hours of the day. Just enter things as they happen. You could do it by hand or in your contact manager. It has a timer, so establish a "Company" called "Time Wasters" and "Contacts" for each day. For some, keeping it as a piece of paper in front of them keeps them focused when the next time-waster begins. Whatever works for you is the best way. It's **your** map out of the time morass.

Can You Combine Goals?

To spend more time with family, can part of a project be done together? For instance, if mailing products or information is a part of the process, can your family help? Kids can stuff envelopes or boxes and attach stamps.

I've used postage meters and haven't seen the value in them. Ditto for online postage. If any of your mail weighs over a pound, you have to take it to the post office anyway, or be there when your carrier comes to hand it over. So why contribute to red ink in your financial statement by paying a premium for the red ink in postage meters?

The family that works together...

While working together, you can catch up on what's going on with your family. If you have to make deliveries or trips to the post office or UPS, schedule them so you and the family can do something afterwards. Just getting out of the house is hard when you work at home. If you combine the time it takes to do a business task with a personal task, you will actually save time.

Ron is a self-publisher. "I wanted to spend more time with my family, but found that the business of writing, publishing, and selling my own books consumed an enormous amount of time. There were a lot of steps and I couldn't afford to hire someone to do them. Then it dawned on me that we could make it a family project. My kids and I work together packing, addressing, stamping envelopes, and taking orders to the post office. It's like the old days when a family worked together on a farm or in a small store."

This brought the family closer together and made the business profitable. You can do something similar with your business.

If you're in a relationship, your partner (who still works outside the home) will often ask you to go to the drug store, take the kids to soccer practice, etc. Combine those tasks with business tasks.

Make a Schedule—
Don't Weave a Straightjacket

▸ Remember the Big Picture whenever you schedule something.

▸ Make appointments with yourself—for yourself.

Focused Time Gets More Done Faster

Make your schedule work around your natural rhythm. If you are at your best bright and early, use mornings to do the most work. If (like me) you are a night owl, make your business work around that, if at all possible. Some research indicates that those with ADD tend to have a harder time focusing in the morning, but that groggy trait isn't limited to them. You may be a day person, but not an early-morning person.

How do you find out your productive hours? Simple. Keep a short diary in chunks of three hours, morning and afternoon. Write how you feel and briefly what you worked on. For example: "10 a.m.—Wow! I'm really on fire! Finished bang-up spreadsheet for new product line." Or, "1:00 I just can't get into it. Maybe I should take a nap. Worked on Johnson proposal." After a couple of weeks, you will see a pattern and after a month you will know for sure what's best for you. Be more concerned with what you **feel** than what you **did**. Most of us are so task-oriented that we don't think of how we feel about doing things. When we are self-employed, we should be able to manage our time more in line with what is best for us, not our imaginary stern bosses, judgmental bosses, father-figure bosses.

If the Johnson proposal was so bollixed up that Johnson followed up with an e-mail suggesting you get into some sort of rehab program without delay, you'll have a pretty good idea that 1 p.m. is not your best time of the day.

Once you know your best hours, utilize them for your most challenging work. Use the least productive hours for mundane tasks, like filing, decluttering, opening mail, or talking about routine matters on the phone. When we talk to others, we get immediate input that can energize our lethargy.

Saved time is YOUR time.

Schedule trips to office supply and grocery stores before 3:00 p.m. Stores are less crowded and you'll spend less time checking out. You might even stumble across a clerk who knows something and can actually help you. **Spending less time makes time—for yourself.** Always remember that.

Remember to schedule "fun" time.

Psychologists agree that not making time for "fun" is a common failing of home-workers. With the pressures of family and work it's hard to imagine doing something so "unproductive" as having fun. It is important to slip into mental neutral and coast a little bit every day. Don't fill your weekends up with work. It's okay to work half a day on Saturday, if you really feel you need to, but reserve most of the day for fun for yourself and your family. Those hours you've saved by not commuting mean you don't have to work eight hours like you did at the office. Office workers typically unwind and have fun when they come home. You should, too. Once a month, take the whole weekend off. Go somewhere, even if it's only to a local park or museum. Share those saved hours with yourself and your family. Don't worry about being a slacker. Your unconscious will be working on creative ideas for your business.

Why Meditate or Set Intentions?

Meditating and setting intentions are the most important things you can do for yourself. They keep you in balance with your God and your inner self. They recharge you and imbue you with enthusiasm to produce your best work. In meditation, you seek guidance to keep on your path. With intention-setting, **you** decide what you want to accomplish today. Raju owns a travel agency. "Before I even turn on the computer, I spend about 20 minutes setting my intentions for the day before me. I simply open myself up to the Universe and ask for guidance in accomplishing the task I know I will need to do this day. It is not quite mediation and not visualization. It is an opening of my mind to the Universal flow that is all around."

You'll tailor the exact times that fit you, but something like this will make your day far more productive. A schedule eliminates routine decision-making, the boogeyman that steals most of our time. A schedule is a suggestion, not a command. While there are "only" seven hours of real, productive work, they are focused. You don't waste time commuting. Seven focused hours are more productive than 12 scattered hours.

IDEAL SCHEDULE (FOR DAY PEOPLE)		
TIME	TYPE	ACTIVITIES
7-9	Personal/Family	Meditate, exercise, read paper, clean kitchen, start laundry, fix breakfast. If you have kids, add plenty of kid time.
9-10	Business	Set intentions for day. Open for business. Download bank statement. Take messages from answering machine. Check faxes. Reply to e-mail. Open calendar. Print "follow-up" report. Make Doing list. (Schedule mail time according to mail carrier's schedule.)
10-1	Business	Produce heaviest part of business work product. Write correspondence. Answer phone. Produce work from "follow-up" report." Mail?
1-2	Self	Lunch. Take out something for dinner. Get clothes ready for upcoming event. Get ready to go out for errands, banking, sales calls.
2-4	Outside or Inside Business	"Outside" day—get it over with before rush hour. "Inside" day— schedule data entry, return phone calls, mail? Complete outgoing work like faxes, statements, whatever needs to go out tomorrow. Pick up kids. Take to band, soccer. **4:00 is your finish line.**
4-5	Business	**Declutter!** Replace files. Put everything back in its place. Clean office, desk. Prepare it as though you might not be back tomorrow and someone else will have to pick up where you left off.
5-9	Personal/Family	Pick up kids if necessary. Dinner. More housecleaning. Weekly meetings (recovery, self-improvement, social). If single, expand to 10:00. **Schedule some fun time.**
9-10	Personal/Family	Everybody finish what they are doing and get ready for bed.
10-12	Personal	Really free time. Make it sacred.

IDEAL SCHEDULE (FOR VAMPIRES, ER, NIGHT PEOPLE)		
TIME	**TYPE**	**ACTIVITIES**
11-Noon	Personal	Meditate, exercise, read paper, clean kitchen, start laundry, fix breakfast.
Noon-3	Business	Set intentions for day. Open for business. Oddly enough, this time block could be your second most productive time. First check your e-mail. People who e-mail expect immediate answers and if you wait until later in the day, their day is already gone. Respond to voice messages. Check faxes. Open calendar. Print "follow-up" report. Make Doing list. (If mail has already come, work on it right after returning calls.)
3-5	Outside or Inside Business	This is the time you'll have to spend calling people, going out into the world, etc. On the days when you don't have to leave your business, and have few calls to make, it is perfect for outlining projects you'll finish late at night. Do the grunt work now, because this requires attention to details. Save the creative or Big Picture work for your creative hours. Get some lunch. Your lunch time is more flexible than a day person's because you still have to be out running errands during off-peak hours. If you have a family, some of this time will be taken by family obligations. This is just as important as any other part of your day.
5-6	Business	**Declutter** and "not clutter" now. Doing it now will free your desk of clutter so it won't distract you when you really get going. Pay bills, balance checkbooks, file, etc. Create "follow-up" report for next day.
6-9	Personal/ Family	Dinner. More housecleaning. Weekly meetings (self-improvement, recovery, social.) If single, expand to 10:00. **Schedule some fun time.**
9-11	Self	Really free time. Make it sacred.
11-2	Business	This is probably your most productive time. Use it for those projects that really need your creative input. **Make your finish line 2:00 a.m.** You'll probably want a light meal before going to bed.

Some of us left the corporate world because we just couldn't fit into the 9-5 routine. We start a business and what do we do? We put ourselves back into that trap. While much business has to get done during the hours everyone else is awake, it's not mandatory that you be available all day. If you live on the East Coast, and do business in the Midwest or West Coast, it is easier to work odd hours than if you live on the West Coast. Even if you don't get started until noon, it's still morning in the rest of the country.

Turn Your Time Zone Into a Plus

When you leave a voicemail message, do you really expect someone to call you back immediately? Usually, what we are calling about isn't urgent and a few hours won't make or break the deal.

When I moved to California, I feared it would be impossible to run my Internet travel agency with East Coast customers. It wasn't. My voice mail explained I was in California and asked customers to leave both day and evening numbers to reach them. People in the East think Californians are flakes anyway, so they accepted the unusual hours. In fact, it was a plus, because, since I specialized in exotic spa vacations, many people didn't want to discuss mud wraps and de-stressing getaways at their jobs anyway. Fellow West Coasters understood the odd hours.

What If I Have to Work During Regular Business Hours?

Never answer the phone when you are sleepy. Trust me. I found this out the hard way.

If you can afford it, hire someone or an answering service to cover the phones for the first few hours. Even if you have to get back to customers later, they will be far happier if they talked to a person instead of a machine.

If you have to use a message machine, record a message something like this: "You've reached Mike Nelson at Spa World Reservation Service. Our regular business hours are Noon to 8 p.m., PST. Please leave both a day and evening phone, so we can help you."

Special Considerations

Check your phone messages and e-mail first thing. This keeps you from being too out of step with the rest of the world. If you wait until later in the day, it's like responding two days later to day people.

Your creative hours are later, so use them for big thinking.

You keep "regular" hours with your family. This is important. This is the Big Picture.

Summing Up

Whichever hours are the best for you, use them for long-term planning, tackling projects that require a lot of thinking or the most brain-work.

Whichever are the least productive hours, use them for returning phone calls or other non-demanding tasks.

Return phone messages and e-mails the first thing. People expect timely responses. The longer you wait, the more likely it is that they will go somewhere else with their business.

One of the main advantages to having a home-based business is that you can make a map of your workday. Create your schedule around you and not the other way around. By doing the most demanding work when you are best able to tackle it, you actually save time because you are less likely to make mistakes and will get more done in less time.

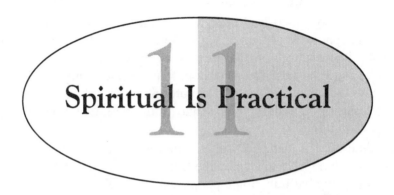

Spiritual Is Practical

Become willing to see the hand of God and accept it as a friend's offer to help you with what you are doing.

—Julia Cameron, *The Artist's Way: A Spiritual Path To Higher Creativity*

Key Concepts

1. Prayer and meditation are different paths to the same goal.

2. You already know how to visualize.

3. Meditation is the next step.

4. You can integrate this into your whole-istic life.

Modern business authors like Stephen Covey, Harvey Mackey, Stedman Graham, and others emphasize that our spiritual and business lives are intertwined. Who we are is not as important as who we are becoming.

The chronically disorganized have let clutter choke their spirituality. If your soul was one wall supporting your house, it would be covered with clutter vines. They wouldn't be beautiful, flowering vines. They would be flowerless, ugly weeds. Their tendrils would dig into your framework, destroying your support. Do you find it easier to pray or meditate in your cluttered office or home or in a church or woods? Clutter takes our attention away from our spiritual life.

Meditation Is the Next Step

Before we begin to declutter, we visualize our desks and offices as clean, clear spaces, as we learned in Chapter 9. Visualization is not meditation, but it is a start. Now that we've seen the practical value of visualizing, we're ready to take the next step, that of meditating. We'll use the meditation techniques in the next chapter about the Shadow Self. Everything we learn is a building block that forms the foundation of the new lives we're building.

Meditation is a loaded word. It conjures up visions of saffron-robed monks. You don't have to assume the Lotus position. Just get comfortable. I meditate in the bathtub. Some people sit with their backs against a wall, or in a chair. **Where** doesn't matter. **How** isn't important. **Doing it** is all that matters.

If the phrase, "guided prayer," is more comfortable, use it. The concept is the same. Prayer and meditation are just different ways of communicating with God. If you are unfamiliar with meditation, use the same relaxation techniques to get into a deeper prayer-state. Instead of visualizing actions, talk to your God about what you want to know.

There's no secret to spirituality. There is no one way to "be" spiritual. You can always grow and become more spiritual, but it's a matter of the heart, not the head. You can't think yourself into a spiritual life. You can't fake it. Who are you kidding? God?

Meditation Primer

Making a daily meditation period part of your routine energizes you, helps you focus and accomplish goals in your personal and business life. At first, 10 minutes will seem like an eternity. Eventually, 20 minutes will be about standard. You don't have to do it in the morning. Whenever you have uninterrupted quiet time will do fine.

I start every day with a short meditation, asking for guidance on whatever projects I may have planned. More importantly, I ask my inner, authentic self, to speak to me through the day to keep me on track. It's like having a personal coach with me through the day. My authentic self will tell me when I am doing things that are outside its paradigm. It doesn't chide me, or blame me, it just asks something like, "Is this what we want to do?" At first, you'll confuse your inner-self-talk with inner-guilt-talk. The difference is that your inner self will not ever say "should" or make you feel guilty. It will be gentle.

Close your eyes and relax.

Breathe slowly, deeply, through your nose. Pull the air all the deeply, all the way down to the bottom of your lungs. You'll know you've done this right when you feel your rib cage expanding at the very bottom. Exhale from the bottom of your lungs by contracting your stomach muscles and pushing the air back up through your lungs, and out your slightly open mouth. You should both feel and hear the exhalation.

Do this several times until you feel pleasantly relaxed. Release the tension in your neck by rotating it left to right, right to left. Shrug your shoulders, imagining them touching your ears. Let all the tension leave you. To relax even more, imagine that waves of relaxation are flowing through you, like ocean waves rolling to the shore as you inhale. As you exhale, see those waves rolling back to the sea. Using your dominant learning skill, you may want to visualize the word "Relax," in front of you, or hear the ocean flowing through you. You may wish to chant (silently or in a low voice out loud), "Relax," or "Peace," or whatever word feels right to you.

Feel each area of your body, your neck, chest, abdomen, thighs, legs, feet, relaxing in turn. (If you get distracted, merely note it and move on. Let the distraction evaporate like smoke.) When you are sufficiently relaxed, feel yourself sinking into your chair, the floor, or wherever you are. Your body will be supported. You don't have to put any effort into maintaining your body.

Go inward to your quiet, calm center. You can visualize yourself as a light beam going deeper into the center of your body. Deeper inward. Direct your vision to your day ahead. (Whether you do this in the morning or evening, it's good to look forward). Ask for peace and guidance on living this day according to the principles of your life. You may get visions of specific actions, or you may just get feelings of "doing the right thing at the right time." Other people may be part of them: family, co-workers, bosses, strangers. Whatever comes to you is authentic. Notice the feelings that dominate. If a person with whom you are having a conflict appears, bless them and bathe them in a glow of warm, loving energy. You will be amazed at how they become less of a challenge in the real world. This may happen immediately, or it may take some time, but their negative energy will dissipate and your conflicts will dissolve.

Make these feelings real. Pull them into your inner self. Make them part of you. What you have done on this spiritual, psychic level is real to your inner self. Make those feelings strong enough and you can call them up during the day whenever you lose focus, or get angry or scattered. Sometimes you can do this immediately and sometimes you'll need the brief visualizations below to help you.

When you feel ready, slowly return to the room and sit for a moment with your eyes closed. Feel yourself integrating with your surroundings. Slowly open your eyes and take on your day, or have a peaceful sleep.

Spiritual Exercises to Heal Rebellion

**In my workshops, this concept resonated with the participants
more than anything else I said:
We clutter because we are rebelling.**

Psychologists tell us that rebellion and disassociating from our parents at certain ages is necessary for us to define our own self. Those who did this successfully defined themselves, moved on, and dealt with other challenges to becoming an authentic person. Those of us who didn't are stuck with a need to rebel. Our cluttering is sometimes a manifestation of this thwarted need to define ourselves.

Along with the Shadow Self exercise, this is the deepest work we can do to effect permanent changes in our cluttering habits. Experience has shown that there are other reasons for our cluttering that we will have to keep working on, but if we work on this we will improve dramatically.

At work, we will silently rebel when our bosses give us an assignment, saying under our breath, "Nobody's going to tell me what to do." Then we procrastinate, do the project poorly, clutter our desks, or misfile documents. Even if we maintain order at work because of fear, when we get home, we refuse to clean up our mess, saying, "It's my house and I'll do what I want." This is all unconscious, because we don't want to own the fact that we are acting out teenaged behavior.

Inherited clutter is the symptom of this in our personal lives. This subject has come up on every talk show I've been on. It's the hardest to deal with. I've dealt with it myself. This brings out the issues we haven't dealt with regarding our parents. These issues are within us right now. We just ignore them. These conflicts don't just appear when we inherit our parent's old clothes. Cluttering is never about things. It is always about people.

We are going to deal with those issues right now. Living or deceased, we are going to constructively rebel against our parents. We are going to get out of this clutter trap.

We are going to make peace with our parents, deceased or living. As *The Course In Miracles* says, "It is a required course. Only the time you take it is voluntary." You will confront this issue. If not now, when?

You aren't alone and you aren't crazy. Go to a quiet place where you will be assured of no distractions. Go back into a deep meditative space as explained earlier in this chapter. When you have reached your inner, calm center, concentrate on the person(s) you need to talk to. They will appear. Greet them with love. Look them in their eyes. The first step is to forgive them.

It is unimportant whether they dominated you through their own insecurities, ignorance, or just because they were doing the best they could. Blaming them and continuing to rationalize that you are right and they were wrong is unhealthy for both of you. It maintains this unresolved dialog.

Using your own words that will come naturally, say something like:

"I acknowledge and appreciate your loving efforts at raising me. I am not denying you, or negating what you have done for me. I accept that you thought you were doing the right thing. We both succeeded, because I am now grown. But somewhere along the line, I wasn't able to really define myself and learn how to do things my own way. I listened to you and took on your values. This has caused a great conflict in me, and rather than learn to create my own values, I just went along with your judgments instead of causing you pain by confronting you.

"Today I am starting over. You have your life and have no reason to hold onto me. By letting you go in my own mind, I am letting you go in your own life. You don't want to be shackled with my life nor do I with yours. Today, let's set both of us free.

"Today, I am a teenager. Today I begin to question those things that you told me I 'should' do. Today I begin to ask myself what I want to do, what I want to be. It will not be easy, but I will refrain from asking your advice or opinion.

"I accept that I will make mistakes. I accept that I will have to learn the hard way. But it will be **my** way.

"You only wanted the best for me. I am sure that you didn't know the stress I have created for myself. I know you love me and want only the best for me. I know you want me to have a happy, fulfilled life.

"I know that I have your blessing to go forward and create my new life. God bless you."

If you've done this exercise successfully, you should feel a sense of peace and liberation. If you don't, try it another time. It may take several attempts. Please do not give up.

When you are ready to come out of your meditative state, very slowly, very gradually come up to consciousness.

Whether you talked to the living or the deceased, you have changed the energy of the relationship. You have psychically changed the dynamics. In a very real sense, you have changed the brain chemistry of your self-talk surrounding your parents.

Now that you've done this, what are you going to do with it?

You are going to learn to live an independent life. It's over. You are both released from the old contract. Dependant people make no decisions. You are going to take responsibility for your life and decisions.

Short Visualizations to Get You Through the Day

Whenever you feel the need to refocus, close your eyes and repeat one of these short statements. They work hand-in-hand with your deeper meditations:

1. Thank you, Great Spirit, for this perfect day ahead of me. I know You will give me plenty of time to accomplish the tasks that are necessary, and the wisdom to know which they are.

2. I close my eyes and breathe the air of beauty and harmony that surrounds me. I go to that perfect place in my soul where the angels of neatness honor my presence. They love me and offer me their help in those times when I feel that I am alone. I am never alone. These angels are always beside me, guiding me, helping me. God's love is always with me. His angels are my constant companions.

3. My work is an expression of my Godliness. Throughout this day, I will honor my God by creating harmony where there was discord, order where there was chaos and clarity instead of confusion. Clutter keeps me from seeing my true purpose. Clarity of purpose keeps me from cluttering.

4. Oh Great Spirit, who created all things, teach me to honor and cherish Your works. Teach me to respect what you have made by giving all my possessions the care and attention they deserve, not by hiding them or otherwise dishonoring them. All that I

have has been given to me by You, and I strive to show my gratitude by cherishing each item. If it contributes to my business success, I will give thanks. If it has outlived its usefulness to me, I will eliminate it. If it is worn out, broken or useless, I ask your help in discarding or recycling it, so that it may return in another form.

5. I visualize life as an enormous circle, without end or beginning. As I travel around it, I see that the road ahead is clean, orderly, and happy. If I look backward, and see the disorder I have left, I do not feel shame. That was but one point on my journey without end. I see the future as an unending series of points of clear lights, clear thoughts, clear spaces. Outside this circle that is my life, there are larger and larger circles, millions of them. They are the journeys of my fellows. Where we touch, we bring strength and harmony. My circle is one of many, not unique. If I have strength, I share it. If I am at a weak spot, another circle rushes to my aid. God's love is infinite. It is through others that He expresses it. Today I will be an expression of perfect order and calmness. Tomorrow, another may take my place. Circles within circles, lives within lives, we all touch and support each other. I am never alone.

Follow Principles in Your Life and Principles Will Help You

No matter what religious or spiritual teachings you follow, take some time to learn more about them. Reading the Bible, or the writings of Tao, Buddha, Ernest Holmes, Marianne Williamson, Billy Graham, or whomever speaks to you will center you. Going to church can fortify you because of the power of being around people of like mind, as well as learning from a teacher who has spent the whole week on a 30 or 40 minute lesson to help explain things.

If you have a family, what better way to be close together than going to church? If you are single, what better place to meet someone of value? Staying centered in today's world takes effort. Staying centered pays big dividends. It is a better retirement plan than a 401(k).

The Shadow Self

*Those who would have right without its correlative,
wrong…do not comprehend the great principles of the
universe nor the condition to which all creation is subject.
One might as well talk of the existence of heaven
without that of earth, or of the negative principle without
the positive, which is clearly absurd.*

—Chuang Tzu, Taoist philosopher

In my work with clutterers, the one thing that helps the most in awakening is a glimpse of the Shadow Self. Although this is a deep psychological concept, pioneered by Dr. Freud and clarified by Dr. Jung, today many psychiatrists have accepted that we all have Shadow Selves and that confronting them is part of the path to wholeness.

Edward C. Whitmont M.D., was a founding member of the C.G. Jung Institute in New York, and he defined the shadow thusly, "The term shadow refers to that part of the personality which has been repressed for the sake of the ego ideal." The following is not a complete examination of our Shadow Selves. It is a clarification of what the Shadow Self has to do with our cluttering behavior.

We generally think of the Shadow Self as the embodiment of tendencies like greed, intense anger, unfaithfulness, murderous rages, or other seriously "bad" actions. We keep them in check to fit into society. Yet, these very dangerous qualities come out in seemingly normal people with regularity. We all have a shadow, or many, shadow selves. Our cluttering is a relatively benign expression of one of them. While it seldom results in the deaths of our co-workers, (unless we suffocate them with paperwork) it does kill our self-worth. In a sense, we are burying ourselves with papers and decisions not made. We are killing ourselves slowly.

We've all heard about religious or political leaders who live exemplary lives, doing all the "shoulds." Their public lives embody the lighter self that we all aspire to. Then, a shocking expose reveals that they have been living two lives, that they were secretly womanizers, pornography addicts, child molesters. The mild-mannered accountant skips the country with embezzled funds. What happened? Because they never confronted their Shadow Self, only repressed it and denied it, it broke out vehemently. That which we repress will always come out in negative ways.

The Shadow Grows

When I was a little boy, an image was indelibly imprinted on my mind (visual learning). I was told to imagine my soul (visualization) as a clear glass of milk. My soul was white and pure. I need to point out that white has nothing to do with race. When presenting this concept to workshop participants of many races, no one objected to the word "white," as we all have been taught that "bright white light" is a source of goodness. Black is beautiful in people, but as a color, black in our culture universally represents the embodiment of evil. So please don't get hung up on some politically correct semantics.

So we are all born with this white-milk soul, or a pure colorless soul. As we grow, we learn that we "shouldn't" do certain things. "Good little boys don't pull little girl's pigtails." "Good little girls don't turn around and slug boys who pull their pigtails." "Good children don't fidget." "Good children turn in neat papers." "Good children pick up their rooms." As we did certain things that were "bad," our milk bottle turned gray when we did little "bad" things, and eventually turned black when we had done enough of them. If we did one really bad thing, like hating our parents, our glass turned inky black.

Some psychiatrists have compared the shadow self to a backpack we have strapped onto on our backs through life. We start out with an empty pack, but as we learn to be socially acceptable, more "ought to" (good girls and boys do this, not that), we fill it up with the pack up with the "shouldn't have" ("Bad Boy/Girl" things we secretly would rather do). Carrying them around and suppressing them takes our energy. The pack gets heavier and heavier, and our aching shoulders scream for us to let them out. Sometimes, we let one out, doing something that is unlike our normal character.

We feel the great power of the "bad" things and are either repelled by them, so we work harder to repress them, or we delight in them and keep doing them. We take the negative consequences of the actions and pervert them into a reward. We *want* to stop, but we can't. If the actions are relatively benign, like cluttering, we can get away with it our whole lives. If they are the darker shadows, like theft or murder, we become sociopaths and eventually get caught or killed. This negative reward is the only way we can quit this spiral if we truly give into our deeper, darker selves. That is why we fear our shadows so much. We fear that they have unlimited power over us. But, we will learn that they don't. They have only the power we give them. And we will take that power away.

We do our best to fit in, to be "good little boys and girls," and we repress all the "bad" parts of our personalities. We **should** keep our desks neat. We **should** be on time for appointments. We **should** file **properly**. So we repress our desires to do things the way we want.

Why Do We Do These Things?

> "That which we do not bring to consciousness appears in our lives as fate."
> —C.G. Jung

An overwhelmingly common clutterer trait is rebelliousness. We rebel against all these "shoulda's" and clutter in opposition to them, or to the people who tell us what to do. In effect, we let this Shadow Self run rampant. We feel like we are unable to do anything about it and just suffer the consequences. We have a convenient scapegoat. "The devil made me do it," so to speak.

We aren't cluttering because we want to. We are cluttering because that which we are afraid of in ourselves is forcing its way out. We are getting back at our bosses, our spouses, our parents, at all those who told us we shouldn't do certain things. We are turning into the things we hate, thus hating ourselves. We know we "should" be neat and organized. We feel like we can't. So our cluttering lowers our self-image. We feel we can't control this behavior. We feel like failures.

Even the criticism of our cluttering comes from the Shadow Self— other people's. You can easily determine what your shadow qualities are. Just imagine someone you don't like. Write down the personality traits you detest about them. That which we hate in someone else is what we fear in ourselves. The perfectionist has a strong dislike for clutter and clutterers. She actually fears them, because not-neatness is part of her Shadow Self. She fights it, afraid that it will come out in her.

In a sense, clutterers are mentally healthier. We know what our shadow looks like. We have given in to it. That makes it easier for us to confront it and deal with it.

Let's Do Something About It

> "When we attempt to deny what **is**, to deny such things as the natural cycles of time and space, enormous energy is required."
> —W. Brugh Joy, M.D.,
> a teacher of Heart Centered Transformation and Spiritual Enlightenment (*www.brughjoy.com*)

The more we deny this Shadow Self, the more energy it takes from being productive. Our goal is not to deny our shadows. They are part of us and always will be. Have you ever embarked on a self-improvement process and been surprised when, just as you got one of your less desirable habits under control, something else you'd never noticed popped up? It's like we are playing a children's game where we have a flat surface with several holes. A round peg is sticking up. We hit it with a hammer, pushing it out of sight. This makes another peg jump up somewhere else. So it is with our personalities. By knocking something down, denying it, we push it below our consciousness. It's not gone, just not visible. It, or something else, will jump up into our consciousness somewhere else.

We need to meet our shadows and take their power from them. We have to do it on their level, beneath the surface.

Will the Meditation Technique Work for Everyone?

It can. Anyone can meditate. Anyone can do the following exercises. But some of us won't let ourselves. We may have so many blockages and locked minds that we don't believe we can. We may be too intellectual. Some people even believe meditation to be non-Christian. Pray instead. "Guided prayer" is a Christian concept that defuses disbelief. Use the relaxation techniques and imagine yourself talking to God about your dark side. Forcing yourself to "meditate" when you feel uncomfortable with the word will be counter-productive. Meditation is listening. Praying is asking. Visualization is seeing. They are all paths to our goals of an integrated, spiritual life.

Even for those of us who know how to meditate, this exercise may be difficult. We are delving into an untouched part of our psyche, combining the spiritual and psychological. The two are not exclusive, but we may think so. Don't force yourself. When you are ready, you will return to this chapter. You will be amply rewarded.

> "It takes nerve not to flinch from or be crushed by the sign of one's shadow, and it takes courage to accept responsibility for one's inferior self."
> —Dr. Edward C. Whitmont.

Meditation Technique

Use the techniques described in Chapter 11 to get into a meditative physical state. Instead of directing your vision to the day ahead, go deeper into yourself. This will take longer and you absolutely have to have about 20 or 30 minutes of uninterrupted time.

When you are totally relaxed, imagine that you can see your soul, your inner being. Within that space, you will see two beings. One is a small, bright-light little boy or girl—your pure, childlike nature. Some people need a more concrete image like a Casper the Friendly Ghost figure. This is your real self, your non-cluttered self. You will sense happiness and cheerfulness emanating from this child.

The other being you will see is larger, darker, more powerful. Some imagine a dark angel or Darth Vader. Whatever you choose is immaterial. There is no "right" vision. Just see something that, to you, is dark and evil. This is your Shadow Self. In this sense, it is your cluttering self. It embodies the emotions and rebellions that manifest themselves as cluttering.

You'll probably sense fear. Do not be afraid. This is part of you and cannot harm you. The shadow self fears you. It is afraid that you are going to deny it, crush it. It is ready to fight you.

Defuse that fear for both of you. Tell your shadow something like this, using your own words:

"I see you and I love you. You are part of me and I respect that.

You are necessary for me to be real, to be whole. I value you."

With practice, soon you will sense a lessening of fear, both in you and in your shadow.

"I do not deny you. I respect your right to exist. You provide an anchor for me to judge my actions. But, you have been alone here in your dark corner too long. You have grown, absorbing all the power around you. Today, we are going to share that power. We are going to take some of your power and give it to our lighter self. You see, the lighter self is part of you, too, just as you are part of me. We won't take all your power, just enough to help us all live better lives."

Bring your lighter self into focus:

"You are my lighter, brighter self. You want to shine and radiate goodness, clarity, an uncluttered life. Today you are going to absorb some energy from our shadow self and transmute that to white light energy. Today, you will be the stronger self."

Visualize electrical lines joining the two. Imagine power flowing from the dark self to the lighter self. **See** the electricity sparking and running from the dark to the light as bright blue streams of energy. **Feel** the energy flowing. As the energy flows, **watch** the lighter self grow in size. **See** the dark self shrinking. **Sense** it losing its power. As the lighter self grows in power it grows in size. Soon it will be 10 times the size of the dark self. The dark self will have shrunk to a very small entity. Stop there. Do not imagine it completely disappearing. This will anger it and cause it to react strongly. It is just as much a part of you as your lighter self. Let it live, just don't let it dominate you.

When you are ready, when you feel that the lighter self is strong and powerful, gently say goodbye to each of them and gradually come up a level in consciousness. Stay relaxed for as long as you want, and reflect on the feelings you now have about yourself, but don't open your eyes or return to complete consciousness.

Most people who have done this with me are very relaxed, very confident, and feel buoyant. They feel physically lighter. It's as though they were carrying around a heaviness they didn't even know about. This is what you were meant to feel like. Revel in it.

Put This New Self to Work

Now, you are ready to really work on your cluttering habits. While still relaxed, go into the visualization mode. Visualize those areas that bother you the most. **See** yourself working through a stack of papers, cleaning out  your files, decluttering a room, whatever you want to do the most. As in the visualization exercise, use all your senses. **Hear, feel, sense** the actions as if they were really happening. Feel the weight of each paper, hear it rustle, hear the file drawer open, feel the weight of it as it slides forward. Be particularly aware of the sense of accomplishment, success, joy that you get as you make decisions on what to file, what to toss. If a shredder is part of your visualization, feel the rumbling it makes, hear the humming, feel the papers being sucked in, watch the ribbons of paper going into the waste basket. Hold onto these feelings. Make them part of your consciousness.

You will be able to tap into these feelings when you actually do the work you envisioned. You will be able to do these things effortlessly in the real world. For what you have made real in the psychic sense becomes real in the physical sense.

When you've finished the task you've chosen, gently, slowly, return to the physical plane. Spend a few minutes reviewing what you just did. Accept it as real.

If you are at home, or have a home office, you could go and immediately do the project you just visualized. You will be astounded at how easy it will be. Congratulate yourself on your success. Reward yourself with something meaningful.

Will It Always Be This Easy?

No. Our Shadow Self will grow and come back with time. We can practice this exercise whenever we feel this happening. Once you have done it, however, it becomes easier and less time-consuming to relegate it to its place. After a time, you will be able to do it at work (with your door closed and phone off) in a few minutes. You've created a "state." You can return to this state quickly, now that you have the map.

As you become more comfortable with this technique, it is likely that you will eventually want to meet your other shadow selves. That is part of a growing self-awareness that learning about our cluttering starts. Some words of caution: Some of the shadowy parts of our selves are harder to deal with. If you encounter something that is just too uncomfortable to deal with, **stop**!

The process may start you on the road to seeking out a psychiatric professional. That's a good idea, as most of us cannot deal with the deeper parts of our personalities alone.

For more understanding of the Shadow Self, Dr. Brugh has workshops listed on his Website. My old, friend David Richo (*www.davricho.com*), presents workshops in California and does individual counseling. The book, *Meeting The Shadow, The Hidden Power of the Dark Side of Human Nature*, edited by Connie Zweig and Jeremiah Abrams, is a magnificent compilation of articles on the Shadow Self by many experts, including Dr. Carl Jung. When you are ready to work in this area, you will find it fascinating and rewarding.

Depression

In the Shadow Self meditation, you may meet other children who are very unhappy. As I have in the beginning, approximately half of us suffer bouts of depression. Several people in our meetings have read, *I Don't Want To Talk About It, Overcoming The Secret Legacy of Male Depression* by Terrence Real. This book is on the cutting edge of what we know about the causes and treatments for depression. If you have been dancing around the edges of calling a psychiatrist for a diagnosis, this book can save you a lot of valuable therapy time, even if you are a woman.

It's About Time

*People will go to enormous lengths—diets, exercise
programs, magical cures, reading books;
they'll do anything before they'll revise their schedules.*

—Dr. Larry Dossey, M.D., lecturer and author of *Healing Beyond The Body* (Shambala Press, 2001), *Reinventing Medicine* (Harper, San Francisco, 1999) and other books. Dr. Dossey was a pioneer in the belief that time-related anxiety contributes to myriad physical disorders.

Key Concepts

1. Slow down.

2. Turn your vagueness about time into an asset.

3. Don't fill every minute with "To-Do's."

4. Plan your day with the Big Picture first.

Hurry, hurry. Rush, rush. Get more done faster. Multitask. Be more efficient. Make better use of your time. Don't waste time.

Bah humbug!

Ralph Keyes, in his book *Timelock* (Harper Collins, 1991), said, "The futile hope underlying self-imposed time pressure is that by living it fast and cramming it full, we'll get more out of life. In fact, we get less that way.

Slowing down and uncluttering our lives not only allows us to better enjoy our time, but to get more done." (For more wisdom from Mr. Keyes, visit his Website *www.ralphkeyes.com. Timelock* is perfect for clutterers and other who want to break out of the time trap. His most recent book, *Whoever Makes The Most Mistakes Wins: The Paradox of Innovation* (with Richard Farson, Free Press / Simon & Schuster, 2002), offers many insights into the way innovation works).

Time/Efficiency Addicts

Time addiction is like any other addiction. Being addicted to living by the clock means making the clock a god. The rush from always performing, always beating the clock is like the rush from snorting cocaine. Take deadlines away from time-junkies and they go into withdrawals, just like drug addicts.

A cocaine addict said, "When I use cocaine, I feel like I can make things fit in the time between the time. I can get more done, faster and better."

Does this sound familiar? Do you want to cram 48 hours of work into 24? Instead of drugs, you expect proper time-management to transport you to this false nirvana.

Time? What's That?

Clutterers are on the other extreme of time-consciousness. We are vague about time. That's probably a good thing. While we need to ratchet ourselves up a little bit to get into step with the rest of the world, I don't think we need to become obsessed with time. Finding a happy balance will do just fine, thank you.

When we cram too many things, too many "To-Do's" into a day, it is like borrowing from a high-interest credit card. Like the Biblical story of the brothers who got an equal inheritance, we can squander it or use it wisely. Whether we bury it or invest it in ourselves, we never get more **quantity**. What we do get by using it effectively is more **quality** of life.

Those at the Top Understand Time

> "To begin to understand your relationship with time or clutter, understand the deeper level. What do I gain? [by cluttering or appearing time-stressed]. Poor me. Help me.

Being pressed for time makes me look like I'm a very important person. A lot of time leaders, CEO's, people at the top are more relaxed about time than middle managers. Understand your need to be more relaxed about time."
—Ralph Keyes

Use Your Sense of Time to Your Benefit

As a clutterer, you have a different sense of time. Honor that. Instead of making *time* finish lines, try to make *project* or *task* finish lines. Use your vagueness about time to your benefit. Don't try to become a square peg in a round hole. Make your schedule around yourself, instead of wrapping yourself around somebody else's clock. There are times when you will have to be punctual. The airplane won't wait for you. The Type A client won't tolerate you arriving at "nine-ish."

Your use of time is one way others judge you. Time awareness is as much a part of your personality as your good humor, your compassion for others, and all the other positive qualities that people judge you by. Personalizing time makes it easier to deal with.

"About Time" Is Your Way of Keeping Time

"About" time means rounding time down to the next logical break. Arriving "about 9 a.m." could mean 15 minutes or 29 minutes earlier than the appointment time. This doesn't mean adding a specific number of minutes to each appointment. We all know people who add 10 or 15 minute to their watches. That works for awhile, but eventually they factor in those extra minutes and it doesn't help them one bit.

When you have to be on time, own the schedule instead of letting it own you. If your plane leaves at 2:18 p.m., tell yourself it leaves "about 1:30." If it takes 45 minutes to get to the airport, say it takes "about an hour and a half." Always double drive time. The variables of traffic are beyond your control, but scheduling extra time is not. That appointment at 9 a.m. sharp becomes "about 8:00 or 8:30 in the morning." (You will learn how much extra time you need to give yourself the more you do it). Start adding about an hour or so.

There are no hard and fast rules. **You** are making **your** time schedule. That report due on Friday becomes due "before the end of the week." The key word is **before**. Thursday is just as before the end of the week as Friday.

The Longer Away the Due Date, the Easier to Err

When I have a book project due, I make the finish line approximately a month before it is due. I haven't yet turned a book in a month early, but haven't ever been a month late either. Long before they are due, **double-check long-term due dates**. I lost a month on this book. When I checked the contract, my "about" time was actually **after** the real due date. "About" time saved me from getting an irate call from my publisher a month early in Mike-time. Double-checking the contract earlier would have saved me from many long nights of rewriting under a **dead**line instead of coasting effortlessly towards a **finish** line.

De-stress Commitments

I drove 12,000 miles, presenting 15 seminars in 12 cities coast to coast, last year. I'll do the same thing this year. I wasn't late for a single one—more importantly, wasn't stressed out by time. Imagine a clutterer saying that after two-and-a half months on the road! Recovery has its rewards.

If people pay good money to attend a seminar that starts at 7 p.m., they expect it to start on time. I told myself I needed to be there "about an hour early." It takes about 30 minutes to set up, but it could be done in 15. If I arrived early, I used the gift of extra time to meditate and center myself. I was assisted by wonderful volunteers who helped set up, but allowed time to set up by myself in my calculations.

If you give presentations, always assume everything will go wrong. Giving yourself time to check the details makes you a better presenter. Try to arrive the evening before, instead of the day of your presentation. Even organized presenters have horror stories about not having something crucial and not having time to fix it because he arrived "just in time."

Due Dates are Really "Due by or Before" Dates

Finish lines are when something **has to be** out of our hands. Things are due, or appointments are "by, or before, a certain time." Your MasterCard bill is not due **on** the 15th of the month. It is due **by** the 15th. If you pay it on the day the statement arrives (which is variable), you'll be less stressed out trying to meet the due date.

The same holds true for everything else we do. Instead of time causing you stress, make it give you a bonus. When you arrive early, you have "found" time. Instead of cramming something else into that empty slot, savor the space, like the clear space in your bookcase. Use "found" time for thinking about the Big Picture. A few extra moments spent thinking about how you want your life to turn out will pay more rewards than shuffling papers. Even daydreaming will pay off more than trying to get something else "important" done. We need to replenish our imaginations. Instead of detracting from your effectiveness, it will add to it. Some of the best ideas come when the mind is floating free.

You will probably start arriving early. What? An early clutterer? Isn't that an oxymoron? It used to be. But you are entering a new paradigm. **You are making time work for you, instead of making it the enemy.**

Take Your Time, Don't Let Time Take You

"I am in a hurry. Please take your time." Napoleon, said this to his tailor. Mssr. Bonaparte knew that the value of doing something right the first time saves time, even if it takes longer.

It may take you longer to finish projects than other people. That's okay, as long as it isn't an excuse for procrastination. Procrastination means putting a task off as long as possible. Taking your time means doing something correctly, even if slowly.

All of us know our astrological sun sign, even if we don't believe in astrology. I am a Taurus. As a child, I remember reading descriptions of the "traits" of bulls like me, wishing I were something else. Taurus was described as "methodical," "slow," and even in one book, "rather slow to learn, but can be trained to do most tasks, given enough time." Gosh, I really wanted to be an Aries when I grew up. They were decisive, bold. Geminis were at least quick-witted and good talkers.

In business, we have exalted the traits of Aries and Gemini. We look down on those who don't scurry about and "get things done." We want everything to be done right away.

How often have you done a report rapidly, or had one turned in by an employee, only to have to have it redone? How often is the quick answer the wrong one? A three-minute egg isn't made any better by cooking it five minutes, but it is equally ruined by cooking it two-and-a-half minutes.

Take your time. Do it right. You don't have time to do it again.

Do You Know Where Your Time Goes?

When I interviewed Mr. Keyes, he said, "A significant growing minority of people are simplifying lives. Especially true since 9/11. Once we examine what really matters to us its amazing what we spend our time on. Ask yourself what's the reward for being in motion all the time? What's the reward for an overfilled calendar? Do I really thrive on stress? You have to get to the real questions."

According to the Bureau of Labor Statistics, the average American worked 34.5 hours a week in 1999. I'd like to meet this slacker. He probably has 2.3 kids, too.

Deduct an hour for lunch even if you eat a sandwich at your desk. That leaves seven hours. At your best, you are going to be 80 percent productive. That leaves you about five-and-a-half hours to get real work done.

We are not automatons. We take breaks. We get calls from our family or friends. We have to go to the bathroom. Most traditional organizing systems don't seem to take that into account. Thus, we are set up for failure. If most of us were truly productive for five hours a day, we would be heroes.

Wait, you are thinking, am I advocating that we turn into a nation of slackers? Not at all. I am advocating that we find our pace and work to it. Most of the great writers and thinkers worked about six hours daily at the most. Most of us are lucky to have two to three hours of really effective productive time in a day.

Sure, there are days when you work nonstop, fully concentrated on the tasks at hand (a positive application of hyperfocusing). You seem to accomplish 10 hours' work in a seven-hour day. Good for you. Most of us don't keep that up for more than a few days at a stretch. (Sure, we hear about lawyers, programmers, or engineers who work 15-hour days to prepare a case or complete a project. Then they get some sleep and settle back into a routine of slower motion. Our bodies are not meant to work on adrenaline forever. Either we give it a break or it breaks). Some people do maintain schedules like that and they burn out. I respectfully suggest it is better to chill out than to burn out.

If you regularly get 80 percent of what you want to get done in a day, a week, a month, you will be more of a success than the person who gets 110 percent of his goals achieved for a short time.

Allow about 20 percent of your time to focus on the Big Picture. It is less stressful than trying to accomplish 20 "have-tos" on your Doing list. It's also the most valuable part of your time.

Overachievers will pack more things into their Doing lists than the average person. That is their pace. Too often we equate doing more with getting more done. Doing one or two important things in a day is more effective than crossing out 20 relatively minor "accomplishments."

Final Notes on Time

I don't wear a watch. Neither does Ralph Keyes. He was the first person I'd read who suggested eliminating timepieces. I physically cannot wear a watch, due to a rare condition in which the nerves of my wrist are too close to the skin. I insisted on wearing one, even though it hurt, because I thought it was the adult thing to do. Mr. Keyes freed me. I haven't worn a watch in 10 years. And, once I started using the "about" time method, haven't been late very often. There are always clocks around us; Our cars have them, the radio stations tell us. Train and bus stations have them. I've asked people on the street the time and no one has ever said no, even in foreign countries.

A watch encourages us to be exact about time. The old watches with hands at least gave us some latitude. Do you really care that it is 3:22? About 3:30 is good enough for me. I feel more free without being shackled by a timepiece.

For years, I didn't even use an alarm clock—even when I was working at real jobs. I learned to tune into my body clock and to visualize the time I needed to wake up. Alas, I've lost that ability, except when I take naps. I work late and sometimes have to get up early (before 10 a.m.). Fear has made me return to having an alarm clock. Nobody is perfect. But when I nap, it is just too much trouble to set an alarm for 20 minutes from now. I visualize the time I want to wake up and do so. Maybe I will trust myself to use that for getting up in the morning again. Try it, preferably on the weekends. If you can get comfortable with waking up naturally, you will find yourself waking up happier and less groggy.

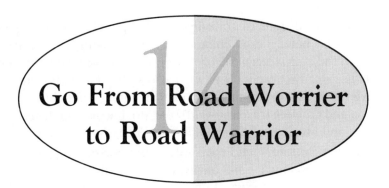

Go From Road Worrier to Road Warrior

Is there anything as horrible as starting on a trip?
Once you're off, that's all right, but the last moments are
earthquake and convulsion, and the feeling that
you are a snail being pulled off your rock.

—Anne Morrow Lindbergh

Key Concepts

1. Your trip starts before you leave.

2. At last! A cluttering trait comes in useful.

3. The rule of three rules.

4. Your trip doesn't end until you unpack—and pack for the next one.

Ah! The traveling life! Remember when you thought that traveling on business was going to be fun? Remember imagining staying in fancy hotels, eating high on the hog on an expense account and meeting interesting people on planes?

So now you are older, wiser, and road-weary. Today, with the extra security measures, traveling has become even less fun. Believe me, I've been there. And sometimes I still have to go there. Let's take the trip together and make it less stressful and more organized.

I've Been There

I've talked to dozens of traveling businesspeople and have paid my dues to join this beleaguered community. In my youth, I was a traveling salesman, in the days when we drove from store to store with our samples. (I sold ladies' ready-to-wear). I flew cross-country doing publicity for the Mexican government, promoting my books, and doing trade shows. My most interesting and grueling traveling was by car, driving the length and breadth of the U.S. and Mexico, writing guidebooks. Yep, I've been there.

I've known clutterers who have solved the decision-making dilemma by taking an empty suitcase and buying everything they need upon arrival. They end up with a lot of extra clothes and toiletries which just makes life harder once they get back.

The return part of your trip is just as important as the beginning. We'll deal with unpacking a little later on, because we don't want to start with the hard part.

Stress

Traveling causes stress. Stress causes cluttering. Cluttering causes stress. Taking too much stuff causes stress on both ends of the trip. Deciding what **not** to take can drive a clutterer to the looney bin.

The reason clutterers have such a hard time with traveling is that it requires far more decisions in a short amount of time than staying at home and going to work. To make the traveling life work for you, eliminate as many decisions as possible.

"Dr." Mike sez...

℞

Use these aids for packing stress. Take as necessary before trip.

Reduce the number of decisions.
Pack early.
Keep suitcases partially packed.
Have a travel wardrobe ready to go.
Keep travel size items in suitcase.
Use clear plastic bags for like items.
Unpack and return luggage to storage.

It Starts Before You Walk out the Door

Your trip actually starts before you ever leave home. So does the stress. If you wait until the last minute to pack, you are bound to forget something, lose sleep, and operate on less than peak efficiency. Fortunately, there are some simple solutions that actually appeal to clutterers.

Here's Where a Cluttering Trait Comes in Handy

Clutterers tend to have two or more of everything. Then we feel guilty about it. Here's permission to have two of everything you'll need on your trip. We have two suitcases that are just for traveling.

I've counseled clutterers to use short "Doing" lists in general, but traveling is a situation when a long list is essential. Using your favorite list-making method, begin compiling a checklist of everything you normally take on a trip.

This is where length, breadth, and creativity can run freely. Make a master list on your computer, so you can reprint it when the old one wears out. Group categories such as: Clothes, Grooming, Medicines, Gadgets (we have plenty of those). Make sub-topics for each individual item. Be as specific as possible. Include everything you want to take, then eliminate as much as you can. Ask yourself, "Do I really need this?" As you travel, check off things you use. When you get back, if you haven't used something, eliminate it for next time. One gadget I've found indispensable is a steamer for clothes. It is lighter than an iron and works as well. While hotels may have irons, you can't count on getting one when you need it.

SAMPLE CHECKLIST						
CLOTHES	#	GROOMING HAIR	EYE	MEDICINE	GADGETS	COMFORT
Shirts, Blouses		Brush Spray	Drops Shadow	Prescriptions	Computer: Programs, Floppies,	Coffee Tea
Pants, Skirts		Shampoo Condi-	Mascara	Pain relief Lotions	CD's, Phone	Reading CD's
Suits, Dresses		tioner		Tooth- brush	cord, Ext. cord	
Ties				Tooth- paste	Sound machine	
Socks, Hose					Ear plugs	
Dress shoes					Steamer for clothes	
Casual shoes						
Underwear						
Raincoat						

The list functions several times in the traveling situation. It reminds us what to pack, eliminates the stress of decision-making, and helps with the stress that we are going to forget something. Now pack the list. Now. Before you have plans to go anywhere.

Keep a copy in your luggage (taped to the inside top) and in your purse or briefcase. When you move from hotel to hotel, check the list as you pack.

Use lots of heavy-duty plastic bags to hold like items. It's easier to pull out a bag of underwear that to root around for a pair of socks hiding under a stack of folded clothes. Keep your grooming gear together and pop it in and out of the bag instead of scattering it all over the dressing counter. You will be less likely to forget a razor hidden under a towel when leaving.

Work with this list. Add new items, delete what you never use. Keep it updated. Have several copies to have handy for a quick trip.

Carry any medications and a pair of underwear and socks in your brief-case if you check your luggage. Get medications partially filled in small bottles. Just putting them in a bottle that didn't come from the pharmacy is risky. You might need to know the dosage and type of medication, plus a pharmacy bottle has the phone number on it. You never know.

If you just have to have a certain brand of shampoo and a conditioner, get two heavy-duty plastic bottles. The metal ones are really better, but if you are going to carry them on, plastic will save you a lot of aggravation at the security checkpoints. If you're going to check your luggage, by all means get the metal bottles (available at The Container Store, Bed & Bath and other specialty stores.) The plastic ones seem to be targets for disgruntled baggage handlers. Put bottles, even the metal ones, in a plas-tic bag to confine leakage.

Many of people swear by those hanging organizers with compartments for toiletries. I've used them and find that they take up too much room. I swear by plain old baggies.

The Rule of Three

Keep three changes of underwear, socks, t-shirts, etc. in your big bag. Keep one set in your overnight bag. Why a set in the overnight bag? How often has a day trip turned into an overnight trip because of canceled flights, late arrivals or because new things came up at the client's that could be solved the next day? Have you ever tried to find underwear in a strange city? Sure, you could buy more, but then you'd have more clothes clutter when you got home.

Keep three extra changes of clothes just for traveling. Keep them packed. Since we have such a hard time with making decisions, have the decision of what to wear already made for you before your finish line of departure. Taking those items to a laundry, long before your next trip, is a great idea. They will look better when you arrive and having them nice and neatly folded will discourage you from making any changes. An extra suit or jacket and pants should always be packed and ready to go.

That's really about all you need to conduct business and have a hassle-free trip. The more stuff you take with you, the more clutter you'll have in your room, and the more trouble it will be to pack.

I always carry three sets of ear plugs, because they are easy to lose. Bright-colored ones are best. Keep them in a small plastic bag. The wax ones are useless, as far as I am concerned. Foam ones fall out. The best are cone-shaped and spongy. Sleep masks are handy both in the room and on an airplane. If I have to fly, I keep both the mask and ear plugs in my coat pocket. It's the only way to really nap well on a plane for me. If you do this, have a water bottle handy, as you'll miss the drinks and wake up dehydrated.

Can You Drive?

With the inconvenience of flying these days, consider taking a train or driving. The advantage of a train is that you have much more room to stretch out, it's less stressful, and you can really get some work done on the way. If you add up the time it takes you to get to the airport, go through security, get your bag, and rent a car, you may find that it's about equal, time-wise, to taking the train.

Driving offers clutterers more opportunity to take their "stuff" with them. Doggone it, I like having my stuff with me. It provides a comfort factor. At least I no longer carry my portable Jacuzzi. I drove 12,000 miles giving seminars one year. I got to take my expresso machine, my special coffees, and changes of clothes for the different climates I'd en-counter. Combined with the flip-chart, tripod, video camera, still camera, etc. that I really did need, driving made much more sense. While you can't get much paperwork done driving, that is why God invented cell phones. Oh, I know it's politically incorrect to laud cell phones, but if you get a decent headset, you really can get work done while you drive on the open road. I conducted three media interviews while driving.

Use the same checklist as above when traveling by car. Have an additional one for car stuff: tools, jumper cables, tire chains, flares, and so on.
Auto stores have useful gear bags. Don't forget a coffee mug! An advantage of driving is that you can take your own pillow. If you take your own
pillow, use a distinctive pillowcase. But don't forget to put it on your checklist. I lost a few before I perfected this system.

Mapping Software

Reduce your stress, whether driving or flying, by knowing where you're
going. In a pinch, Mapquest maps will work (*www.mapquest.com*), but
they are horrendously inaccurate. AAA's *Map N Go* is fine for long drives
and knowing where the Interstates are, but forget city maps. My favorite
software is *Street Wizard* by Adept Computer Solutions
(*www.streetwizard.com*). Not only are the maps accurate, but they can be
downloaded to your PDA, work with GPS, and are published to the web.

If you give seminars as I do, this is a huge bonus. You can publish your
locations, and add driving directions and notes on your Website. Another
feature I really liked about them was their use of landmarks. *Streets USA*
will put in a symbol for a church, but *Street Wizard* will tell you the name of
churches, schools, parks, and other landmarks that locals will know. Thge
copy to clipboard (as GIFs) feature is unique (even *X-Map Business* pub-
lishes as bitmaps). You can use them in Web pages.

DeLorme makes a mapping program *Street Atlas USA*, which is okay,
but lacks the details of *Street Wizard* and isn't publishable to the Web.
Their high-end product, *X-Map Business* will map your database contacts
from *Act!, Goldmine, Excel*, and is publishable to the web, but now that
Street Wizard integrates with *Act!*, I suggest sticking with it. It does have
the names of parks and landmarks, which is a good feature.

Street Wizard Version 8.0 competes with Delorme's *X-Map Business*,
which works like a charm. Like *X-Map Business*, it plots data from *Excel,
Access, ACT!* and *GoldMine*. *Street Wizard Pro* goes a step further and
links directly with *ACT!* and *GoldMine*. Right from *ACT!*, you can ask it
to plot any group of contacts on the map. (If *Street Wizard* isn't open,
ACT! will automatically open it.) Then, if you see a contact on the map
you're interested in, double click it. You'll automatically switch back to
ACT! and the chosen contact will be displayed as the current contact.
This tight integration between *Street Wizard* and *ACT!, GoldMine,* and
others makes it the choice for *ACT!* users. *X-Map* has pwoerful drawing

tools, a phone directory, and demographic information. *X-Map* displays by region (unless you copy seven Cds to your hard drive).

Both will work with your GPS, which can come in really handy for drivers. There are others, but avoid any that use *Mapquest.com* interfaces.

Your Laptop

If you have one of those really nice, expensive laptop carry cases with lots of foam padding, pitch the padding. It only adds weight and takes up space. Unless you're planning on dropping your laptop, they are overkill. Be sure to carry your Windows startup disk. You probably don't need many program disks, but make sure of that before you leave. Mapping programs are usually happier if they can find the maps. Put CD's into the newer, thin jewel cases. What a wonderful invention. Once again, use your detailed checklist for computer gear you'll need.

Having what you need and makes you comfortable is not clutter. Working on the road is tough enough without having to adapt to cramped workspaces. I like a trackball and hate touch pads. For me, it is worth the extra space to carry a trackball. There are some tiny ones made for laptops, but I never could get used to them. Be sure to have a long (25 feet) telephone cord, with a double connection on one end. You may want to work on your balcony, or on the bed instead of a teeny-tiny desk. A 12-foot extension cord will give you plenty of freedom. Be sure to have some blank floppy disks or CD's, depending on whether your laptop still has a floppy drive or a CD-burner. If you need to print, there are some really nice, small printers today that will fit in your laptop case if you get rid of the extra padding. And, yes, that extra battery takes up space and weight, but can be a lifesaver. Whatever you think you'll need, put it on the list. Then check it off if you never use it.

If Your Office Is in the Car

> "I keep my car neat and organized. I can find any customer's file is seconds. Most insurance salesmen's cars are a mess. They throw files in the back seat and waste valuable time searching for them when they visit a client."
>
> —Tom Sullivan, agency manager

When I was a traveling salesman, it was a nightmare to keep the car decluttered and my contact information together. On my nationwide tour, now that I am less cluttered, I discovered nifty ways to keep things (and my serenity) together.

Hanging plastic crates are perfect for filing. They are square, stackable, and you can see what's in them. Put a box, preferably wooden, in your truck to hold them. Do not put them in your back seat. The first emergency stop will scatter them everywhere. A small hanging file box with a lid is good for your immediate appointments. Don't try to cram everything in there. Transfer files from the crate in the back as you need to. Put the already used files back in the crate.

Get a plastic drawer-box for odds and ends. I have to mail books and kits while on the road. I put all my mailing supplies: tape, scissors, stapler, envelopes, FedEx labels and envelopes, and paperclips in there. I only unpack it only when I have things to mail. I have a small box with a lid containing a stapler, paperclips, and tape for regular work to be done in the hotel room.

Make one crate with items you have to carry into the room each night, so you don't have to unpack everything every night. Don't mix your personal stuff with the business stuff. Even if it means an extra box in the trunk, you will feel better looking for business items there than rooting through your suitcase.

Getting a Good Night's Sleep

If you don't sleep well, you'll have a cluttered mind. There is no way to insure you'll get a quiet room. You can insist on one with the reservations clerk, but that seems to work about as often as flipping a coin. If you make reservations online, forget it. I am a very light sleeper and here's what has worked for me. Don't waste time telling the 800 number reservations clerk. You can type it into comments online, because it might help to have something in writing. Get the local phone number of the hotel. Call and tell the desk clerk what you want. Make a point of getting his name and tell him that you will personally pay him to put you in a quiet room. Five dollars might do it, but no more than 10. I learned this traveling in Mexico and it works fine here in the U.S., too.

If you can stay with the same chain, you will be more familiar with what you are getting. That means a lot in reducing stress. I have found really good deals and pleasant surprises with independent motels, but there have been about as many unpleasant ones. Hilton Hotels (when you can afford them) offer dependable quality and familiarity, as do Holiday

Inns. I am more likely to be found in the Red Roof Inns, Comfort Inns, Howard Johnson's, and Econo Lodges. Despite their name, Econo Lodges generally have large rooms and decent furnishings for less money. Red Roof has rooms with real computer desks! Not all of the locations have them, but they are certainly a plus.

Reservationists usually don't really know what a quiet room is, so you have to be specific. If you are staying in a hotel with a bellman, you are in luck. These guys have actually been to the rooms and, for a fiver, can fix you right up. You want an interior room in a large hotel, not facing the street. A courtyard is ideal. In a motel you want a room on the end, in the back of the parking lot. First floor rooms have less street noise than second floor rooms, but you get the early morning and late evening traffic. Second floor is quieter than third. People think higher is better. It isn't. Being next to an elevator doesn't bother me, but some people hate it. Personally, I prefer it, since it is usually shielded from traffic noise and keeps you from having another room on one side.

I love rooms with Jauczzis, but try not to get a room next to a Jacuzzi suite. Jacuzzi users tend to be night owls. I always make sure my room has a bathtub. A hot bath after a long trip can be a real life-saver. And, if you're like me, it's a great place to meditate.

As soon as you arrive in your room, check out the air conditioning/ heating. It should be loud enough to mask noise, but quieter than a B-52. It's easier to change rooms right away than it is later. Pack three clothes-pins to keep the drapes together. Even in the nicest places (except in Las Vegas), they never seem to completely close. A thin shaft of light can keep you from sleeping.

Even with the best precautions, you will get burned sometimes. I checked into a marvelous hotel near Boston one night and it was a big quiet room on a corner and away from the street. A group of college kids took over the floor and had a party. I called the front desk and they did nothing. I called the cops and they threw the kids out. Sometimes you have to take care of yourself. Don't delay. Those things don't get better with time.

Today there are white noise machines on small clock radios. They don't take up that much space and will pay you back the trouble of carrying them and then some. Get one with a battery backup. Do not ever trust the alarm clock in the hotel to be accurate. I've seen them set to 9:00 a.m. when it is 9:00 p.m.

Put two or three neon-colored dots, from an office supply store, on your appliances.

Trade Show Clutter

If you are working at or attending trade shows, you're going to come back to your room with sacks of brochures and sales materials. These are mostly clutter. I try to pick up as little as possible and pitch what I get foisted on me before I leave the floor. There never seems to be enough trash cans at these shows, so I leave a pile of them by the front door. There are people who are paid to clean up. Let them earn their keep.

Back in the room, I immediately pitch the fancy folders and pretty brochures. All I keep are fact sheets and really pertinent data. Gifts like mouse pads, and t-shirts. I leave for the maid with a note and a tip. Business cards should be entered into your contact manager right away, but nobody does that. At least keep them together with note scribbled on the back as to who the person was (use your dominant learning skills to describe them) and date the cards.

Carry a notebook or your PDA and take notes when you're talking to people at the trade show booths. Put business cards into a plastic card holder with clear pages. I found that a three-ring binder with several clear plastic pages was perfect for the little useful information I needed to collect. For the rest of the year, I referred back to that binder and always found what I was looking for. Make an index as you go. You can clean it up later.

Coming Home and Back to the Office

I know you are tired when you get home. You want to throw the suitcase in a corner, put your feet up and relax. Don't. Your pre-planning must include time for unpacking and data entry. It is a part of travel. Immediately unpack. I unpacked my truck after a three month trip within an hour of coming home. If you don't do it now, you won't do it. Put your traveling laundry in a separate location from your regular laundry. You've already made the decisions about what to take, so don't mix everything up and make it harder on yourself the next time. Take what needs to go to the dry cleaners the next day. It is another part of your travel schedule.

Refer to your list as you unpack and make notations on what you needed and cross out things you didn't use. This helps keep the list a working document. Clean and put the "ready to go" items back in the suitcase.

Traveling will never be completely stress-free, but if you follow these guidelines, you will find yourself cluttering less and being more at ease.

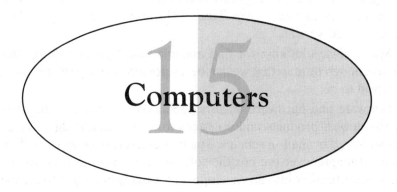

Computers

The solution is not throwing away a tool and grabbing a new tool. It's thinking through what you are doing. People who hated the Palm Pilot loved the Blackberry PDA. It's thinking through what tool you have and finding out what you like about it and what are the challenges about it and coming up with a solution. Tools are made for different people.

—K.J. McCorry, (*www.officiency.com*) Professional Organizer and Spokesperson for National Association of Professional Organizers

Key Concepts

1. Before you buy, ask how much better is better.

2. Everything has a clutter price.

3. If it ain't broke, don't upgrade.

4. There will never be a hard drive big enough for everything you want.

The "Improves Efficiency" Trap

Just as clutterers can be seen wandering glassy-eyed in "organizing" stores buying two of everything to "organize" their clutter, they can be spotted staring at software packages in computer stores. We are suckers for buzzword phrases like "Saves Time," "Improves Efficiency," "Twice as fast as the old version."

We're always looking for that magic bullet, "the one thing" that will save us enough time so that we can be as efficient as we perceive the rest of the world to be.

Software and hardware makers depend on us. We are the ones who buy the newest products and upgrades to try to get an edge. We are the ones suckered by mail-in rebates. The manufacturers know we will lose the receipt (though never the box the software came in) or procrastinate putting the rebate offer into an envelope and actually making it to the mailbox before the expiration date.

Here's an e-mail I received from an admitted clutterer:

"Instead of simplifying my life, computers have complicated it. I buy new machines all the time. Faster processors require newer motherboards. New video cards aren't compatible with older machines, or don't work as well. So, I keep buying new machines. But I can't get rid of the old ones. They seem to have value. It would be a shame to throw them away. So now my house is cluttered with computers and computer parts."

Especially in home businesses, we think we have to have the newest and biggest to compete with the big boys. Laptops; PDAs; newer, faster processors; bigger hard drives; faster scanners; DSL; CD-RWs—these all compete for our attention.

The Software Trap

Compete is the operative word here. Before we actually buy a product, we agonize over it. We read reviews online (we can't find them in our collections of computer magazines). We read the boxes. We put competitive boxes side by side in the store. If we order online, we download trial versions of each product. We spend more time deciding which 99 dollar pieces of software to get than we do choosing a college for our kids.

You don't have time to evaluate every software title. Most of the "new" features are things you will never use. Learning a new program takes time. Installing a new program, all too often, leads to a software or hardware conflict. Those new features are frequently buggy.

Software manufacturers have to release an update every 12 to 18 months to compete. Instead of spending time to make things more reliable, they pack new features into their products. Once it's in your hands, they let you do the troubleshooting and let them know what doesn't work. Then they issue an update or a patch.

Before you update any program, go to their Website and check for fixes and updates to the version you have. The short answer to all software decisions is that we only need upgrades when the new version adds features you really need. New versions always say they will make you more productive. Don't fall for it. Invest time in decluttering, and you'll gain far more productivity. Some computer experts only buy every other version of programs. It usually takes two generations to make significant improvements to most software. Most of the upgrades are little more than window dressing.

Ask yourself these questions before any software or hardware purchase:

1. Is there something wrong with the old one?

2. Does the new one really solve problems for me?

3. Before blithely answering "Yes" to the above question, make a list of the problems it will solve.

4. Do I really need all the added "benefits"?

5. How much "downtime" will be used by installing or learning how the new software/hardware works?

6. Could I use that time better in getting rid of some of the computer junk or old software clogging my current system?

Clutterers are like agent Mulder in *The X-Files*. We want to believe. We want to find an outside solution that will make us more productive. We like to buy things. We are suckers.

Beware the "3 for 1" or "Free After Rebate" Trap

Assume it's tax time. Here's a situation where we have to have a new version of software. So off to the computer store we trundle. Today, the number of tax preparing software programs has dwindled to three major ones. So it would seem like our choice should be easy.

Aha! Those wily software makers know that we clutterers are suckers for "more is better." So they intice us with "Professional" and "Extra Platinum Professional" versions. But wait—there's more. When we buy one manufacturer's version, we get three other products thrown in. And, just to make sure they get us, they throw in a rebate we have to mail back, so we get their product for free!

Admit to yourself that you'll never mail it in. So, throw that out of the equation.

Next is all the "extra" software. While comparing tax programs, I was nearly suckered in by the bonus software for 99 cents. I looked at the three free programs and asked myself if I would have bought them at any price. The answer was "No." They were simplistic versions of things I already had.

Oh, you will immediately say, "But if it does one thing better, it is a bargain at that price."

Wrong, byte-head. Everything has a clutter price. The software will take up room on your hard drive. And before you smile condescendingly and think, "I have a 60 gigabyte hard drive. Plenty of room," think for a minute. When I got my first hard drive, I went for the 30 megabyte drive, even though DOS could only recognize the first 20 megabytes without partitioning. More was better. Twenty megabytes seemed like a lot. Now there are programs that take up more room than that. I got one of the first gigabyte drives. That seemed like far more room than I could ever use. And on it went. There will never be enough hard disk space for everything I want. But there will be plenty if I don't fill it with junk. Keep putting garbage programs onto your 60-gigabyte drive and you'll need a two-terabyte drive.

How to Make What You Have Work Better

Declutter those files on your hard drive. Run Scandisk and Disk Defragmenter weekly. Delete programs you don't use by using their own "delete" feature or get a good decluttering program like *Fix-It,* or *Norton Cleansweep.* Back everything up before running them, as they sometimes delete stuff you don't want them to, but overall, they are safe. If you are running Windows XP, make sure you have the latest versions of these programs.

If you are considering "upgrading" to XP, you should be aware that some older hardware will not work with it, although there are drivers online for some of the products. Also, XP sends an inventory of your system to

Microsoft when you install it, to prevent piracy. You have to buy a copy for each computer in your office. I have nothing against that, but if you upgrade your system more than a few times, XP will not boot. It will "think" you have installed it on a new computer. Microsoft says you can call them and explain the situation, but it sounds like a pain to me. At this writing, I know of several companies and small business users who have removed XF and gone back to Windows 98, Millenium, or NT, whichever they had to begin with.

Declutter Internet Explorer by going to "Tools/Internet Options/Temporary Internet Files" and click Delete Files. Say "yes" to "Delete All Offline Content." In Netscape Navigator, click "Edit/Preferences/Advanced/Cache." Click on "Clear Disk Cache" button. Then click on "Clear Memory Cache."

Viruses Create Chaos

If you have a virus checker, when was the last time you updated it? You'd be surprised at how many people say, "Huh?" You can update these for free and should at least once a week. Newer versions even do it for you. Be wary of opening e-mails with attachments, even from those you know. Scan every one with your virus software first. Keep backups of your hard drive that are three or four days old and constantly rotate them so you will have a virus-free version at all times. Viruses seem to love to attack on Monday, though there is no real pattern. **Always** update your virus program on Monday, at the very least.

Financial Software

Quicken, Quickbooks, and *Money* have automatic reminders to tell you when to pay bills. If your income is regular, have your bills deducted directly from your bank account. Writing checks through your financial program will force you to record all entries. **Do not** use programs like *Versacheck, My Check Writer,* etc. that print checks from blank stock unless you buy a MICR cartridge for your printer. Also, make absolutely sure that they will print all those squiggly lines in *exactly* the right place. I used to make my own business checks until I got some of them returned as unreadable. When this happens, whomever you wrote the check to marks it down as "NSF," even though that's not the case. Many stores now refuse to accept computer-printed checks.

Most banks offer you the capacity to download your statements directly into your check-writing program. Do it every day. It is almost painless, even for the mathematically-challenged of us. **Backup** your financial data daily, on a separate disk or CD.

According to the IRS, one-third of small businesses incur penalties for incorrect bookkeeping of more than $1,300 annually. Consider an online payroll system like *www.paycylce.com* to relieve you of the burden. Less expensive, and powerful is *Simply HR* by Elibrium Software (*www.elibrium.com*). While this doesn't *do* the payroll for you, it alerts you of potential errors and is available online. It can help you keep on track and is easy to use.

PDAs

I've used PDAs since they were called "organizers." I still have a Sharp OZ-9000 that works just fine. This is such a rapidly changing field that the comparison between models I had planned would have been pointless. Regardless of which one you use, they all have plusses and minuses. Palm has the most versatility in terms of software and probably will for some time. The only really different one is the Blackberry. It is the priciest of the lot, but has internet capability and a real keyboard. For those of us who never liked styluses, it is certainly worth the investment (*www.blackberry.net*). Of course, next week....

A PDA will **not** solve disorganization. Apply the same rules to it as to your paper or computer Doing list. To work, you have to use it and sometimes it is easier to scribble on a notebook carried in your pocket.

Getting Rid Of Old Hardware

"My hardware habit has cluttered up my home office. I love to tinker with computers and even though I know better, I can't get rid of old motherboards, video cards, or hard drives. I hate to throw them away. Isn't there some use for them?"
—Greg, a clutterer

I visited Texas A&M University's Maritime Extension School and saw two large rooms completely covered with junk computers and monitors. Because they were purchased with taxpayer's money, there was a complicated disposal process necessary to get rid of them. The State of Texas is unlikely to change their policies any time soon, but your company can.

Junk is junk. Instead of worrying that employees will abscond with an old computer, open the junk room up for them to take whatever they want. Heck, if you have a few real clutterers, they will clean out your storage area in no time flat. Surely your accountant can figure out some way to write them off and let you get rid of them. They are costing you more in storage fees or lost office space than they are worth.

Rotary International (*www.rotary.org*) will take 486 or better computers and ship them to third world countries. Contact any Rotarian or the Website for details. 1-800-GOT-JUNK (*www.1800gotjunk.com*) can also dispose of them for you, and guarantee that your data will be destroyed first. Gerry Coty, owner of the Chicago franchise said, "We get more calls for this service all the time. Companies don't want crucial data ending up in the wrong hands. We've had companies with a couple to several dozen computers call us."

Local technical schools may be able to use old hardware, but ask first. Goodwill and thrift shops are usually cluttered with them.

Old Programs

How much space is being taken up by your original CDs and floppies of programs that have been upgraded or are obsolete? Don't answer. I know. Keep only the most recent release. The old ones are garbage, but they can be useful to browsers of second-hand book shops. Donate them. If you are lucky, you might get a dollar or two, but the important thing is to get them out of your office. The same goes for the manuals.

Is Your Web Site Cluttered?

The purpose of a Website is to convey information. Pop-up windows, confusing menus, and too many fancy moving icons are clutter. Keep it simple. Every site should be reexamined twice a year to see if it has grown like Topsy. Look at your competition. What do you like and dislike about their site? Then go to yours and apply the same criteria. Web designers like to complicate things. Keep them on a short leash.

In Conclusion

Your computer is your biggest ally in the war on clutter. Give it a fighting chance by keeping it clutter-free. It's easy to forget the computer and concentrate on the cluttered papers you can see. But if you don't declutter it, it will stop working. You can prevent that with regular clutter maintenance.

Feng Shui

I applied Feng Shui techniques and tools...and have been enjoying wonderful benefits ever since. An organized, decluttered office follows one of the principles of Feng Shui. Organizing and Feng Shui really work hand in hand. Whatever can be done to ensure a harmonious flow of energy in the office will help the energy level of the worker. Nothing drains the energy level of an office quite as quickly as clutter. When an office is decluttered, the space will naturally become more energized.

—Nancy Kruschke, owner of Successful Organizing Solutions, *www.SuccessfulOrganizingSolutions.com*

Twenty years ago, discussions of meditation and finding your life's work would have been novel in a mainstream business book. Today they are common. Twenty years ago, no business book published in the U.S. would have a Feng Shui chapter. No business book published in Asia would have been without one. Today, American business is global business. Our culture has changed. We are willing to entertain new ideas, hoping to find ways that work. Feng Shui is complicated and requires years of study to understand and apply. This is just a short discussion of both sides of thought about its efficacy.

A Brief Primer of Feng Shui

Ch'i, Qi, or Chi (chee, pronounced like cheese without the "z" sound) is life-force or natural energy of the Universe.

Classical Feng Shui was developed in China and uses mathematical tools based on centuries of observation, manipulation, and probable outcomes. It incorporates Chinese astrology. Although there are Taoist-like teachings, it is not associated with any religion. To really understand Feng Shui will take work. Without getting into a deep philosophical discussion of the different schools of thought, the recent (about 20 years old) Western adaptation is called the "Black Sect." This form is not used in Asia. Some people refer to this as Black Hat. There is a lot of controversy about this, and if you really want to know more, go to the Websites listed in the Resources. "Eight House," "Flying Star," and "Form And Shape" are the more traditional methods.

You can't just get Feng Shui'd once and forget it. Energies change. A good consultant will check back with you and make minor adjustments without charging more. There are nine periods of time, each lasting 20 years. We are currently living in Period seven, which began in 1984 and will end in 2004.

The goal of Feng Shui (pronounced *phong schway)* is to create harmony between individuals and their environment. That fits in with the goal of this book. It is a technique that may work where others have not been successful. A literal translation is "wind" and "water." The idea is that the essential life forces can be used to create positive energy. The hardest point to grasp is that Feng Shui works with both seen and unseen forces. Thus, although an office might "seem" orderly to an observer, there could be unseen forces that encourage disorganization and dysfunction.

Feng Shui has a growing number of Western adherents. If Donald Trump thinks enough of it to change the placement of one of the doors to his casino, it's worth looking at. Books on Feng Shui are big sellers in mainstream book stores. Clutterers, in particular, are drawn to them. I've gotten many questions about Feng Shui and have been asked why I didn't include anything about it in my last book. The answer is that I was skeptical. It is not an easy concept to pick up and apply. I read a few Fung Shui books and was so overwhelmed with the complications of it that I didn't see how I'd ever apply it to my life. From talking to experts in the practice and those who have used Feng Shui, I now know that it is not a do-it-yourself project. I also know that I was too cluttered to make any use of it.

Some of the principles can be common sense. If you have to snake around your office furniture to get to the door, it makes sense to move the desk. Sometimes that's in line with a Feng Shui principle of allowing energy to flow. If a pile of clutter is blocking you from seeing out your door, it doesn't take a Feng Shui Master to determine that the pile is too high. Alas, it is not all that simple.

Your Building May Be Sick

I asked Paul Darby, a Feng Shui Master based in London, with a worldwide practice (*www.fengshuidoctor.co.uk*) this question: "I believe that people are disorganized because of psychological reasons, which may manifest in blocked energy. Agree or disagree?"

He replied, "I do agree—but the environment—sick building syndrome can be the reason for the blocks and the psychological damage."

So we are in a chicken and egg situation. If the environment is sick, it encourages cluttering. If we clutter for psychological reasons, that could contribute to the building's energy. As the business use of a building changes, the environment changes.

Mr. Darby was called in to change the energy flow with positive results reported by the new tenants. It was once a finance company and had since changed to a lawyer's office. "I have also done psychiatric wings of hospitals where different energies needed to come to the fore—to calm, to support, to energize, to lift, to facilitate change. The use of a building is so very important."

You May Be Too Cluttered for It to Work

**When your clutter is so overwhelming that you can't move freely,
it is hard to even imagine such a radical change.**

People who are severe clutterers probably will not be able to benefit from Feng Shui principles until they get their cluttering under control. As I have said many times, if trying something new seems to cause more stress than distress, try something else. We have many areas of our lives to work on that relate to our cluttering.

Minimalist Stress

I spent a night in a Feng Shui master's house. The minimalist environment affected me physically and emotionally. I couldn't sleep. I was disoriented. I felt like I was about to fly apart, as if there was nothing holding me together. I should say that I do not have agoraphobia. I have jumped out of airplanes and been to tall mountains and gone into enormous caverns where there was no sense of walls. I've brought the experience up at Clutterless meetings and every clutterer but one who had been in a similar situation said they felt the same way. Apparently, we need to have "stuff" around us. It doesn't have to be *our stuff*, but we derive some comfort from "stuff."

I've been to many clutterers' homes and offices. Even when they are operating well in relatively neat surroundings, they have more things around them than naturally organized people. Perhaps we are blocking the flow of energy because we are not ready to receive any more. Maybe at this time in our lives, we can't handle any more enlightenment. Some people who read this book will not be able to meditate, either. We are where we are in our relationship to our cluttering. Take the steps that make sense to you and leave the rest. Those techniques that gave you trouble will still be here when you are ready for them.

Even if you have gotten your clutter confined to neat little boxes, that may not be good Feng Shui, as improperly placed, they absorb energy. It would seem that a visually oriented office with open containers would be more flowing, thus, have better Feng Shui energy.

Clutterers who are ready are more likely to benefit from Feng Shui in their offices than in their homes because we are less attached to our office clutter than our house clutter.

No Place to Hide

In our offices, the clutter is seldom as overwhelming as it is in our houses. There are people who swear that Feng Shui has helped them maintain a non-cluttered working environment:

> "Feng Shui complements the process of organizing an office, especially in the area of getting rid of clutter. According to Feng Shui, stacks and piles stifle a room's 'chi,' or energy. If chi can't circulate, concentration and focus are lost. The operating principle in Feng Shui is 'there is no place to hide.' Things appearing small and insignificant, like an overflowing inbox can have a major impact on your vital energy when you are habitually connected to them. I have used this illustration to motivate clients to accept the

idea of getting rid of clutter. Many of my clients are excited when they are convinced that organizing their space will transform negative surroundings into positive life-enhancing and wealth-generating environments."

—Jackie Tiani, Professional Organizer, Business Consultant (*www.organizingsystems.com*)

Pros and Cons

A Feng Shui practitioner admitted to me privately, "There is a lot of superstition in the practice. Some of the techniques were developed in ancient Oriental times when picking up and moving, or rearranging your door was a relatively minor task. You have to integrate what is practical and ignore that which cannot be changed."

Tanis Evans, a Feng Shui consultant, says, "Classical Feng Shui also takes into consideration how each of the people will probably be impacted by the distinct energy of a given. So it is impossible to make rules for everyone to follow, unless you modify the basic principles of an ancient, mathematically based system. In that case, you get New Age Feng Shui; a generic prescription for creating harmony, wealth, and good relationships, but it's like looking at a bottle of aspirin to cure your headache."

Tanis Evans was a skeptic for years until she studied and applied Feng Shui principles in her own home. Prosperity wasn't flowing, so she made the recommended changes. It made a huge difference in her life and money situation. She is currently a Feng Shui Consultant in Austin, Texas (www.*fengshuitexas.com*). She practices classical Feng Shui and has completed the Masters course as taught by Joseph Yu of the Feng Shui Research Center in Toronto (www.*astro-fengshui.com*).

Choose Your Feng Shui Consultant Carefully

"This practice is as old as Chinese culture itself and anyone who teaches Feng Shui without having a good foundation in classical Chinese thought is like someone practicing surgery without first studying anatomy."

—Dr. Stephen L. Field, Trinity University

There is a lot of controversy among Feng Shui practitioners about what is "true" Fend Shui and "New Age" Feng Shui. To complicate it for the layman, each school has its proponents. A good Website that has both pro and con web viewpoints is *www.qi-whiz.com*. It will take you to sites promoting and debunking Feng Shui.

Paul Darby is a good example of someone having plenty of credentials. Paul is a Registered Consultant with The Feng Shui Society - UK. *wwwfengshuisociety.org.uk*, registered with The Feng Shui Guild and The International Feng Shui Network, a member of the governing body of The Feng Shui Society, Professor of Feng Shui and Oriental Studies at The British School of Yoga, member of The Employment Consultants' Institute.

You Mean I Gotta Move My Door?

Not necessarily. Sometimes only minor adjustments are needed to bring the *chi* into alignment with your goals. It also depends on what your goals are for Feng Shui. If promoting teamwork and a less cluttered environment are what you are after, there may be less to do than if you want a complete audit of how your company can bring in new business and make more money.

According to Feng Shui beliefs, buildings breathe through windows, doors, and hallways. They can't breathe if a "Mountain" of things (walls, furniture, and lots of clutter) is blocking the flow. This could manifest in

more cluttering. People need "support," literally. If your desk is facing a wall, you aren't being supported. Just moving your desk won't necessarily solve your cluttering problem, though. You've got to figure out where the *qi* enters and be diagonally across from that. I've moved desks all over my offices without guidance and it didn't seem to help. There must have been other factors involved.

A Case History

I was fortunate to get both sides of a Feng Shui consultation. Tanis got permission from her client to share the story with us. First, her thoughts: "Some structures do not have favorable door locations if your goal is to attract new customers. I audited a real estate agency with two glass doors at the entrance, approximately two feet apart. One was used for entering, the other for exiting. I found that the energy at the left door was actually causing their business to lose money. I recommended that door be locked permanently, a closed, metal mini blind be hung on the inside of the glass door and the "welcome" mat be removed. The right door now serves as both the entrance and exit.

"Other recommendations included moving one of the three partners to a different office; adding some water features; a chiming, pendulum clock; and a few red items. After three weeks, they reported a very big improvement and then asked me to assess the Feng Shui of their homes. The point of this answer is that each place must be evaluated on a case by case basis."

Now, the results as expressed by the client, J.E. Henry Molina, Realty Executives of Austin (*www.jehenrymolina.com*).

"After Miss Tanis reviewed and assessed our company building, it has revealed a great improvement. We are extremely grateful to her. She gave us an insight as to how our office staff members and my partners would improve our productivity by organizing and avoiding excess clutter. Having clutter can and has disrupted productivity. Mentally, clutter was a weight upon our shoulders during the course of the day. Clutter can also become an eyesore for clients, guests, and our staff. Clutter makes everyone feel quite uncomfortable during the course of the day. Having said this, improving productivity thus improves health and wealth."

Final Words

I asked Mr. Darby if there were cases when Feng Shui principles didn't work:

"Usually, if they don't work, it's because they don't work in the way the client envisaged—a case of getting what you need rather than what you want. Also, if the client only partially follows the report and misses out on some of the 'cures' required—this dilutes and sometimes nullifies the effect completely. If followed to the letter—Feng Shui works, slowly or quickly, dependent on other factors. But businesses, because they have many people involved in them, are the most difficult to get going really quickly."

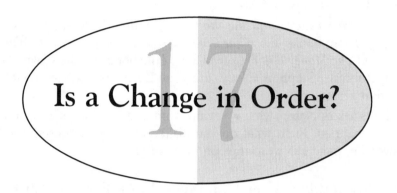

Is a Change in Order?

The Top 9 Reasons Why Clutterers Are Unhappy at Work
1. Have to do boring, busywork.
2. Too much paper to file.
3. No clear priorities.
4. Work takes all time. None left for personal life.
5. Impossible deadlines.
6. I don't agree with the philosophy of my company.
7. Rigid work schedule. I'd like to have some time flexibility.
8. Waste time at too many meetings.
9. Would rather be fishing, golfing, etc.

Maybe You Are Just in the Wrong Job
If you spend much of your working day frustrated and **trying** to organize yourself, maybe the problem is not you. If you've applied the techniques you've learned and they've helped, but you still feel stressed-out, maybe it's just too hard to make your personality fit into the corporate mold you work within.

Running off to get a "better" job, without discovering what's wrong with the first one, won't do any good. Blaming your boss, coworkers, or environment because you can't get organized is fruitless. We don't blame and we don't shame.

So What Should I Do?

Do what you love and the money will follow is both simplistic and realistic. From books like *What Color Is Your Parachute?* to *Do What You Love And The Money Will Follow* to any of the books by Dr. Wayne Dwyer, Tony Robbins, Stephen Covey, etc., you'll find this advice couched in different terms.

Let's ask ourselves what we really want and what steps we can take to make it happen. First, what do you dislike about your present job? The answers on page 195 were tops on my surveys.

Find Something That Combines Your Passion With Making a Living

If number 9 is really on your list, you are in luck. You at least have a direction. Seriously. If fishing (or golfing, tennis, mountain-climbing, computers, etc.) is on your list, then you've narrowed your choices of the ideal job to an industry. That puts you a step ahead of most dissatisfied employees. If you could just tailor your job to something you like to do, some of the other dislikes wouldn't be so unbearable.

No one is going to pay me to fish, you say. Unless you join the Bass Masters tour, or become a commercial fisherman, you are probably right. I typed "Fishing" into *www.headhunters.net* and it came up with 87 matches. Alas, the "Non-Invasive Cardiology Manager" and "Scientist" listings didn't seem too promising, but they came up because the location where this was offered had good fishing nearby. There's a key here. If being close to something you want to do as a hobby contributes to your Big Picture, then finding a job somewhere else really could help.

Fortunately, there was a listing that read: "Hiring fishing reel repairman. Will train". And you thought there were no jobs related to fishing! A hospitality employee at a lodge in the Grand Tetons seemed to offer opportunities to fish as a benefit. "MARINE TECH needed w/exp. for The Fishing Store," seemed more on-target. "MANAGER for recreational facility day fishing, RV Park and picnic area," is right up your alley. A "Communications Specialist for a Recreational Boating and Fishing Foundation" sounded pretty good. The Peace Corps considers teaching fishing skills to be important.

"Golf" fared even better. Of 288 results, the first was a hole in one. "*WomenSportsJobs.com* is currently assisting hundreds of companies, sports franchises, and organizations in the sports industry to immediately fill positions. While we provide a special focus for women, we do not discriminate. All positions are available for both MEN and WOMEN."

The second was for a Customer Service Representative: "Rapidly expanding golf cart parts company is looking for someone with strong customer service skills and a stable working history. Working knowledge of cart parts is ideal, as CSR will be fielding calls from Golf Pros on which parts to use."

The whole point of this exercise is that we feel like we have to make a distinction between what we **do for a living** and what we **live to do**. Maybe we don't. If we are sales managers selling something we don't particularly care about, we could transfer those skills to working in an industry we do care about. Ditto for accountants, secretaries, office managers, computer technicians, and many other careers.

So What About the Other Nine?

Numbers 1 and 2. Busy-work, paperwork.

Instead of interviewing for a job, interview the job. But use the right terminology. Putting "hate paperwork" on a resume or application is interpreted as "highly disorganized." Ask the potential employer how much of your time is expected to be taken up by reports and filing. He probably doesn't know. So ask if you could talk to someone in a similar position. They'll tell you the straight skinny. Career coaches agree that if you can "volunteer" to work for a potential employee for a week, you will get a much better idea of what it is like than by just interviewing. Make friends with someone who works in the same area as your expertise (you might want to take him out to lunch a few times) and find out what things are really like. For this to work, you have to convince him you are not a spy from management, or trying to get his job.

Number 3. No clear priorities.

Every company has a mission statement today. So what? They sound good, but how many companies actually live by them, on the line-worker's level? Years ago, when a major pharmaceutical product was discovered to be tampered with, a line-worker started the process of getting that product off the shelves. That was because the company's mission statement was for real.

Ask your potential boss exactly what you will be expected to do. She'll probably spout something from the policies and procedures manual.

Have you ever read one of those? I've written them for companies and what the bosses thought people were supposed to be doing and what they asked them to do were so far apart that it was like writing fiction.

Ask employees in a similar position what they have to do on a daily basis. Use questions like, "So do you end up working on projects outside your area? Often?"

On the other hand, if *you* don't have clear priorities on what you want to do, how can you expect a job to fulfill them? Take the time to decide what it is you really want.

Number 4. Work takes all my time.

This one is easy to figure out. If the percentage of travel for a job is greater than 20 percent, that alone is going to take time away from your personal life. Ask how many hours someone in your position normally puts in. Be sure to do this in a positive manner, like, "I'm sure that this position requires more than a mere 40 hours a week. I'm used to that. How much time do you think it will take me to do a superior job?" Any boss who doesn't answer that with a real figure is devious. But, bosses being what they are, add 20 percent to whatever figure he gives you.

Number 5. Impossible deadlines.

You'll never get a straight answer to this from a potential employer. Ask others in the same position, or better yet, ask their secretaries.

Number 6. I don't agree with the philosophy of the company.

If you were environmentally conscious and worked for Exxon at the time of the Valdez spill, it would be easy to see why you are dissatisfied. Environmental accidents can happen in any industry. It is what the company does about it that makes a philosophy. You can determine this by doing a little research. If you believe that smoking is a bad thing, you don't want to work for a tobacco company. This doesn't mean that those who work in the oil or tobacco industries are bad, only that careers in these industries might not be for you.

Number 7. Rigid work schedules.

You are probably going to be happier in a job that allows flextime, bonus time for completing assignments early, the opportunity to work from home occasionally. If you are clutterer and have to be at work at 8:15 a.m.

every day, with a coffee break at 10:20 a.m., you are not going to be happy, unless you've changed your attitude about time. There are many jobs that will let you tailor your hours (within reason) to your life. Be sure this is a point you raise with the interviewer.

Number 8. Too many meetings.

It's going to be hard to get a straight answer on this. The number of meetings will wax and wane with every new manager. You can ask the potential employer, "What are the regularly scheduled meetings for the position?" "Do I chair any meetings?" This sounds great to a potential employer. You could follow up with your ideas of how to run a good meeting. You could say something like this if it is authentically the way you feel. Being authentic is part of what we've learned about living an uncluttered life.

The problem is that many meetings are unfocused. Unless there are specific items to iron out, they end up as vague "focus groups." Where they fail is that everyone wants to put his best side forward. Everyone wants to look prepared. I'd like for meetings to have real value.

Knowing How to Make the Right Choices

To help you decide what is right for you, I've asked the advice of career coaches and career counselors. The short answer to the difference between them is that a career counselor will help you determine what is right for you. A career coach will help you find where is right for you.

Although, as I said, most of us do not have AD/HD, we have enough similarities to use advice directed to those who do.

Wilma Fellman, M.Ed., is a Licensed Professional Counselor who works with adults with AD/HD and other challenges, regarding career issues. "I like the three step "Test it out" method that I ascribe to in the book! (*Finding A Career That Works For You*). Wilma offers this advice to people with ADD and clutterers. "If the person tests out potential careers by a three step method—Reading about the potential career(s), talking about it with someone who actually does it, and observe the career in action—more people would make **good** decisions."

Most people first ask, "What are the best jobs for people who clutter or have ADD." As Ms. Fellman said in an article in *Focus Magazine*, said that asking that question is like asking, "What are the best careers for an adult with blue eyes? Perhaps the better question is, what are the best career options for a wonderfully unique individual with special challenges? Let's help them take the time to really get the job done and find what works best for them!"

The same is true for clutterers. Find what type of job suits your learning and organizing style.

How Important Is It?

The following expert has a wonderful and practical approach to determining value. Though she is speaking specifically about employees with ADD, her observations apply to many of the chronically disorganized or clutterers.

Kathleen G. Nadeau, Ph.D. is a nationally recognized expert on Attention Deficit Disorder in adults, and the author of several books on adult ADD, including *ADD in the Workplace, Choices, Changes and Challenges,* (published by Brunner/Mazel 1997). She is a frequent lecturer and consultant on issues relating to ADD in the workplace. Dr. Nadeau is co-editor of *ADDvance Magazine. (www.advance.com).*

She is the director of Chesapeake Psychological Services of Maryland (CPS-MD), in Silver Spring, Maryland, a clinic staffed by mental health professionals who provide psycho-diagnostic testing to evaluate AD/HD, learning disabilities, and related disorders. The following is quoted by permission from an article, *ADD in the Workplace* (posted on the ADD Website, *www.add.org*).

"A woman with ADD was functioning very poorly as an administrative assistant to an executive. She was frustrated with the many mundane tasks of the job, had difficulty arriving at work exactly on time, and sometimes handled problems inappropriately—jumping to a solution rather than conferring with her boss beforehand. Once again, her savvy boss recognized an intelligent, frustrated person who showed many ADD characteristics. A large fund-raising project had begun, in which she showed great interest. Her boss consulted with her, asking if she would rather work on this project instead of remaining in the front office job. She leapt at the chance for more autonomy and an opportunity to use her creativity and problem-solving ability. Her frequent lateness on the fund-raising project was more than compensated for by working long past normal working hours as she threw herself into the project. She was teamed up with a highly organized, detail-oriented person. This employee's organizational skills, paired with the ADD employee's creativity and dynamism, formed an unbeatable team which was highly successful in their fund raising mission.

"The moral—which part of the elephant you're looking at—determines how you'll describe it. If you only look at a tendency to be 10 minutes late, paired with disorganized paperwork, you will conclude you have a less than desirable employee. If you look at their energy, their willingness to work overtime, and their creative problem-solving, then you've got a superior employee. So, instead of bemoaning ADD employees who can't sit still for hours or fill out their time sheets in a timely manner, employers would do better to celebrate the untapped ingenuity, creativity, and energy waiting to be mined by the savvy manager. The employer who creates an ADD-friendly work environment creates a win-win situation. Put an ADD employee in the right job with the right supports and then stand back! You'll be amazed at the motivation and productivity that is unleashed."

Keep your positive qualities in mind before concentrating on the "negative" qualities of being disorganized. Most people can learn to be more organized, but most people who clutter will still be somewhere on the lower end of the organizing spectrum.

Maybe a Career Coach or Counselor Is the Solution

I can personally recommend two individuals, after having talked to them. They understand us. They also offered suggestions to start looking in the right places. Too often we jump from one job we don't like to another because we have tunnel vision. If you decide you want to look for another job after looking through the following thoughts, you might want to consider a career coach. A coach is different from a career counselor. As Lynn Cutts (*www.manageyourmuse.com*) said, "An organizer tells you how to find things. A career coach helps you make your life work." She specializes in creative individuals, sometimes working for corporations, but more frequently looking for freelance or work-from-home situations.

Wilma Fellman is a career counselor who suggests checking a job out before jumping in. She works with her clients to make sure that they are getting into what they think they are getting into. "As a career counselor I like to take the guess work out of it. It is damaging to the ego to try something only to find that it was **nothing** like what we imagined, and then try something else only to get the same results. "I work with individuals, through testing, assessment and exercises like those found in my book. We collect enough information about them and how they best "tick," and from there, put the puzzle pieces together to make good career decisions."

Wilma is the founder of an organization for professionals working with ADD and the author of two books: *The Other Me: Poetic Thoughts on ADD for Adults, Kids and Parents*, and *Finding A Career That Works For You*. She is also on the Executive Board of the Michigan Career Development Association.

You've Got the Greatest Tool in the World

You have unique gifts and talents and, now that you know you are not weak or hopeless, you will be able to use those gifts and talents. You will always have a cluttering challenge, but you will also always have your special gifts of intuition, kindness, and understanding of others. Don't let yourself squander them by trying to fit in where you weren't meant to, or by regressing to your old cluttering habits.

Sorry, *Pogo*—We have met the victory, and it is ours.

Keep It Going

*I've got the book, and it's starting to help,
but my habits were formed over 25 years,
and I think a group of encouraging folks would be
just the help I need.*

—A reader of *Stop Clutter From Stealing Your Life*.

You've read this book. You have found some things that are working for you already. You are jazzed. Alas, it won't necessarily last. If we've spent 25 years doing things the wrong way, the odds are that we will gradually return to them unless we are vigilant.

Jimmy Rasmussen is the President of Hometown Bank in Galveston. He is a naturally organized person, but he hit the nail on the head when he responded to my questionnaire.

Q: How do you motivate yourself to stay organized?

A: "I get frustrated and feel unproductive when I am not organized."

That's the biggest sign that we have lost our way. Once we learn what being organized is like, we will like it.

Telltale Signs That a Reassessment Is in Order

1. I let myself be messy at least one day a week. I make up for it the following day, but it is getting to seem like a chore.

2. I just got tired of doing things the "right" way and stopped.
    Now, my desk is like it was before.

3. I've made some real progress with the mail, e-mail and filing.
    I moved on to improving my goal-setting and seem to have
    hit a brick wall.

4. Thanks to the improved self-confidence I gained by taking
    control, I got a new job. But something's wrong. I don't
    seem to be as organized as I was before.

5. No one gave me pats on the back for my decluttering efforts.
    What's the use? I'm in the same job, making the same money,
    and don't feel like I'm getting anywhere.

6. My office life is under control. But my home is a mess. The
    office principles don't seem to be the same as the office tools.

Having a clutter buddy is your first line of defense. Your buddy will
help keep you on track.

But, a buddy is only a start. We've got a psychological and spiritual
blockage that has formed over the years. We've felt like we couldn't talk to
anyone about it, because, the few times we tried, people just looked at us
like we were crazy. "Just do it," or "Let me get a really big garbage can and
a weekend off, and I'll declutter your office."

Then there is our home. Oh dear, how often have we "fixed" one area
of our life and found another set of character defects popping up? Does it
ever end? Nah, probably not. But, as we make positive changes in more
and more of our lives, the pop-up devils get smaller and smaller.

Ah, but you don't want to go to a 12-Step program that will tell you
that you are powerless. I understand. Seventy-five percent of people who
identify themselves as clutterers are not in 12-Step programs, and don't
wish to be. There is an alternative.

Could the Power of a Group Help?

Clutterless Recovery Groups, Inc. offers a chance to talk about your
cluttering issues without being judged and to get help and support from
others just like you. The following comes from their literature on
www.clutterless.org:

"We are not a 12-Step Program, nor are we affiliated with any denomination, sect, or creed. Our membership is anonymous. While we do suggest that a spiritual approach to cluttering is beneficial, we do not insist on any one way of prayer. We generally hold our meetings in churches of various denominations, libraries, or community centers.

"We help each other, as only those with the same challenges can. We provide each other with insight and support through meetings. We seek to learn new ways of relating to the things in our lives. We seek to free ourselves from the bondage of clutter and learn to live happy, fulfilling, and prosperous lives.

"Our purpose is to provide education and self-help counseling to people for whom clutter is a challenge in their lives. Clutterers have an emotional and spiritual blockage in their lives that keeps them from discarding unwanted items. We sponsor meetings in cities across the United States where clutterers can share their experience, strength, and hope with each other and find solutions to this disorder. There is no charge for participation in our meetings and no one is turned away for lack of funds. We do request donations so that we can pay rent and expenses, but this is voluntary."

What have you got to lose? Only your clutter. Whether your issues are only work, only home, or both (as it is with most people), you'll find a group of people who have no agenda other than to help each other. What a deal!

Nah. I'm a Loner. No Groups for Me.

Groups aren't for everyone. You can do it yourself if you prefer. It is much harder, but you took charge once and you can do it again. Go back to the beginning. Look at your job like you are a new hire. What seems off-kilter to you?

Your job description may have changed. You may have become so efficient with your new ways that you are bored. Maybe it is time to move on.

> "Remember that while you are climbing your mountain,
> there are other mountains, Keep an eye on the next peak.
> Use the valley between to renew yourself."
> —John Gardner

Make Decluttering a Company-wide Project

Just to make it more interesting, implement a competition among co-workers. (If the boss doesn't go for this, try it with one co-worker. Make it a contest. Heck, I can see the day when the decluttering pool will replace the office football pool.) Make a chart, like those ones that show the number of days without an accident for each department. Offer a department-wide bonus (something they really want, not just a plaque) on a monthly and yearly basis. Within the department, give the best declutterer something special—like half a day off. You are going to get far more than that in increased productivity department-wide than the few hours "lost."

Many projects will be completed in under a month. Others will be ongoing and may never be eliminated. A lawyer, doctor's office, or government agency may need to keep files forever. Here is where a top-down, system-wide system needs to be in place. (If your company doesn't have one yet, here's an idea to stuff into the employee suggestion box and win a prize.) Your company should declare clients, customers, etc., inactive after "X" number of months. At that point, their files should be stored in a separate filing cabinet, or off-premises. A yearly cleaning will find these.

I Don't Have Time to Declutter My Files

One of the reasons people clutter up their files is the old risk-reward decision. They think, "If I spend time decluttering the files, I won't look like I'm being productive. Worse yet, because my files are so cluttered, it will look like I am inefficient in the first place. If I spend time on new projects, I'll have something to show my boss at the end of the month and either get a pat on the back or get to keep my job. Gee, which seems like it will do me more immediate good?" The final nail in a clutter coffin is that decluttering is boring and hard work. It involves the "D Word"—decision-making.

Solution

No matter how ashamed you are of your cluttered office, it isn't a secret. Your boss already knows you are disorganized and hasn't fired you yet because of it. Lighten up! Remember in your Doing list that you put "decluttering" as an activity. Remember that we scheduled it before quitting time or before lunch to give you a reward for doing it. You don't have to do it all at once. In fact, I don't suggest that. You will find certain ways your brain works that will not be immediately apparent until you start decluttering things hands-on. Learn as you go.

Time to Get Clean

Remember when you were in college and had "moving" or "painting" parties? You tricked your friends into doing hard manual labor with a couple of cases of beer. (Unless they were like my friends and it took a couple of kegs). Either way, it was cheaper than hiring a professional mover or painter. That won't quite work with cleaning out your files, but the concept is the same. You are going to trick yourself into doing something boring or distasteful with a reward and by making it a game. Almost nobody likes to declutter. There are a few such misguided souls, but they probably didn't buy this book.

Once a month, go through your files (paper and computer). Make it a game. Reward yourself with something for each inch of paper eliminated. Don't forget to count the hanging files! Getting rid of one of them equals 10 pieces of 20-pound bond paper. A file folder counts for four pieces of paper. Be sure to measure your progress before you shred. It's just too hard to put a ruler to all those little strings of paper or pieces of confetti.

Here's to a New Beginning

> *This is not the end. It is not even the beginning of the end. But it is, perhaps, the end of the beginning.*
> —Winston Churchill

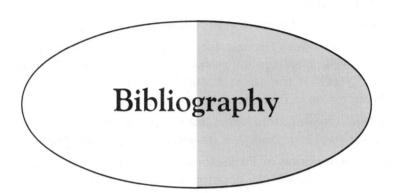

Bibliography

Authors

Covey, Stephen. *The 7 Habits of Highly Effective People.* Simon & Schuster, 1990.

Dossey, Larry M.D. *Healing Beyond The Body.* Shambala Press, 2001

———.*Reinventing Medicine.* San Francisco: Harper, 1999.

Fellman, Wilma M.Ed., LPC. *The Other Me: Poetic Thoughts on ADD for Adults.* Specialty Press, 1999.

———*Kids and Parents, and Finding A Career That Works For You.* Specialty Press, 2000.

Hemfelt, Robert, et al. *We Are Driven.* Thomas Nelson Publishers, 1991.

Jasper, Jan. *Take Back Your Time.* St. Martin's Griffin, 1999.

Keyes, Ralph. *Timelock.* Harper Collins, 1991.

———. *Whoever Makes The Most Mistakes Wins: The Paradox of Innovation.* The Free Press / Simon & Schuster, June 2002.

Kolberg, Judith. *Conquering Chronic Disorganization.* Squall Press, 1999.

Real, Terrence. *I Don't Want To Talk About It, Overcoming The Secret Legacy of Male Depression.* Fireside Books, 1998.

Welch, David A. *Decisions, Decisions, The Art of Effective Decision Making.* Prometheus Books, 2002.

Zweig, Connie and Jeremiah Abrams (ed). *Meeting The Shadow, The Hidden Power of the Dark Side of Human Nature.* Jeremy P. Tarcher, Inc. Publishers, 1991.

Organizations

Attention Deficit Disorder Association (*www.add.org*).

Clutterless Recovery Groups, Inc. Nonprofit self-help group with nationwide meetings and workshops. 1108 17th St., Galveston, TX 77550-6008. $5 for info pack. 800-321-5605
Website: *www.clutterless.org*

Junk Mail Organizations. *http://dnr.metrokc.gov/swd/nwpc/bizjunkmail.htm.* And *www.the-dma.org/consumers/offmailinglist.html.*

National Association of Professional Organizers. Links to certified organizers around the country. Website: *www.napo.net*

National Study Group on Chronic Disorganization (NGSGCD). Links to organizers specializing in the chronically disorganized. Website: *www.nsgcd.org.*

Professional Career Coaches

Colorado, Boulder: Lynn Cutts, Manage Your Muse
Website: *www.manageyourmuse.com.* Phone: 303-449-5411
Fax: 303-245-0250.

Professional Organizers

Colorado, Boulder: K.J. McCorry, Professional Organizer, Spokesperson for National Assn. of Professional Organizers. Website: *www.officiency.com.* E-mail: KJM@officiency.com, Phone: 303-517-5300. Fax: 303-415-9642.

Georgia, Avondale (Atlanta): Judith Kolberg founded the National Study Group on Chronic Disorganization (*www.nsgcd.org*), which consists of Professional Organizers who specialize in innovative approaches for people who have not benefited from traditional organizing methods. Website: *www.nsgcd.org.*
E-mail: worthchat@aol.com. Phone: 404-231-6172.

Illinois, Glendale Heights: Jackie Tiani, Professional Organizer, Business Consultant. Website: *www.organizingsystems.com.*
E-mail: jtiani@compuserve.com. Phone: 630-681-9080.

Kansas, Kansas City: Cynthia Kyriazis C.E.O., Organize It Now. Website: *www.organizeitnow.com.*
E-mail: Cynthia@organizeitnow.com. Phone: 913-649-0878.

New York, New York City: Jan Jasper is a productivity and time-management consultant and highly recommended.
Website: *www.janjasper.com.* E-mail jan@janjasper.com.
Phone 212-465-7472 or 718-435-3199. Fax 509-356-2803.

Pennsylvania, Philadelphia: Cynthia Kyriazis C.E.O., Organize It Now.
Website: *www.organizeitnow.com.* E-mail:
Cynthia@organizeitnow.com. Phone: 215-283-0220.

Texas, Houston: Linda Durham N.A.P.O. Organize It Now.
Website: *www.organizingmatters.com.*
E-mail: linda@organizingmatters.com. Phone: 281-304-0695.

Holly Uverity, Office Organizers Authorized Consultant, "Kiplinger's 'Taming the Paper Tiger." E-mail: Huverity@officeorganziers.com
Phone: 281-655-5022. Fax: 281-655-5030.

Wisconson, Madison: Nancy Kruschke, owner of Successful Organizing
Solutions, Organizing Consultant, Speaker.
Website: *www.SuccessfulOrganizingSolutions.com.*
E-mail: organize@chorus.net. Phone: 608-833-5300 or 866-747-5300.

Licensed Professional Counselors Specializing in ADD or AD/HD Adults

Wilma Fellman, M.Ed., LPC is a Career & Life Planning Counselor specializing in working with ADD or AD/HD adults in Michigan. She is also, "an adult with ADD, a parent with ADD AND the mother of the former poster child for ADD." E-mail: WRZF@aol.com.

Family Counselors

Karen Griggs, MFT, Marriage, Family Counselor, Burbank, Calif.
E-mail: pgriggs@pacbell.com. Phone: 818-761-5855.

Feng Shui Sites and Practitioners

www.fengshuitexas.com. Tanis Evans, Feng Shui Texas, Classical Feng Shui Consultation.
E-mail: tanis@austin.rr.com. Phone: 512-394-9770.

www.fengshuidoctor.co.uk. Paul Darby's Website. Highly recommended as an expert who works across the globe. Headquartered in London, England.

www.fengshui.com.au. If you want to get a start on understanding the different styles of Feng Shui, this is the place to go.

www.qi-whiz.com. Dedicated to helping Fung Shui shed its "snake oil and incense" reputation. If you are skeptical, you will enjoy this Website. It offers both an explanation and defense of the practice and articles denouncing frauds.

www.amfengshui.com. Official site of the American Fung Shui Institute.

Psychotherapists

David Richo PhD. Works with discovering our shadow selves. Lives in Santa Barbara, California and presents workshops around the country. Website: *www.davericho.com.*

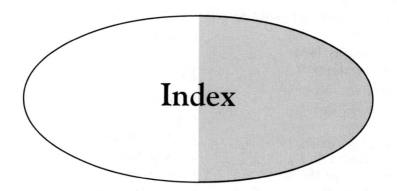

Index

A

Abbreviation trail, 110
About Time, 163
AD/HD, 25, 65, 66
    Is It, 65
ADD, 15, 22-25, 65-70, 113, 131, 199-200
    and Cluttering, 65-66
    in the Workplace, 67
    Personality, the, 67
traits, 68
    counselors, 211
    So, What's It Like to Have, 67
    What Is, 66-67
ADDA, 25
Addicts, Time/Efficiency, 162
An extra file, 105
Approach, Holistic, 32
Assignments, high visibility, 52
Auditory, 45, 120

B

Before and After, 21
Beginning, Here's to a New, 207
Being late, excuses, 52

Beliefs, 61
Better in some areas than others, Why
    are you, 76
Big Leagues, You're in the, 61
Big Picture, 131, 132
Business, 54, 75
    Remember Why You Started Your, 132
Busy-work, 197

C

C.H.A.O.S., 22
Can it be summarized, 103
Car, If your Office Is in the, 175-176
Career
    coach, 201
    counselor, 201
    Development Association, Michigan
        Cartographer, 28
Catalog Clutter, 112
Cemeteries, Deadlines are for, 62
Change in Order, Is a, 195
Changing Habits, 101
Character, 34, 36
Chart, Task Eating Time, 47

Chatter, internal, 68
Choices, Knowing How Tomoku the
    Right, 199
Chronic Clutterers, 30-31
Clean, Time to Get, 207
Cleaning up doesn't last, 72
Clock-time, 34, 37, 68
Clutter,
    Home, how it differs, 135
    is the Culprit, 130
    Phone Message, 113
    Trade Show, 178
Clutterer
    Personality, positive aspects of, 31
    home-only, 49
office-only, 49
    situational, 49
    uncontrollable, 50
    What kind are you, 41
Clutterers,
    filing systems for all types of, 114
    reasons why unhappy, 195
    What Hasn't Worked for, 72
    Social, 30-31
Cluttering Trait, comes in handy, 171
Clutterless
    Recovery Groups Inc., 26
    Recovery Groups, 40
Coaches, professional, 210
Color coding, 122-123
Commitments, De-stress, 164
Company, philosophy, I don't agree
    with, 198
Computer Based Solutions, 115-117
Computers, 179-185
Conquering Chronic Disorganization, 73
Conflicted, Are We, 60
Conflicts, 61
Constrained optimization, 95

Corporations, 113
Create a Safety Net, 104
Creative, 48

D

Day Care Center, Your Office Isn't, 133
Day-Timers, 55
Deadlines, impossible, 198
Decision, You Are Not Your, 86-87
Decisions, only two kinds, 97
Degrees of Cluttering or Disorganization,
    48-49
Depression, 160
Diet, Organizing is like going on a, 23
Directory structure, 116
Disorganization, chronic, 15
Disorganized, mildly, 49
Distracted easily, 70
Does it have to be filed, 103
Doing list, 54, 81
    A Front-line Employee's, 58
    An Executive Manager's, 57
    Keep Simple, 54-55
    My Daily, 56, 57, 58, 59
    Personal Life, 59
Doing, 56-59
Door, You Mean I Gotta Move My, 192
Drive, Can You, 173-174
Driven by Fear, 91-92
Due Dates, 164

E

Easily bored, 48
E-mail, 103, 104
Emotional, 45, 121
Excitement, Creates, 34, 35

F

Failure to Success, 27
Fear
    and Feeling overwhelmed, 19
    is the Enemy, 83
    Is the Root of it All, 83
    of Changing the Status Quo, 87-88
    of Failure, 88-89
    of Making a Mistake, 84-87
    of success, 90-91
    questions to ask, 92
"Feeling" personality, 34, 39
Feng Shui, 8, 187-193
    Consultant, Choose yours carefully, 191
    Master, 22
    A Brief Primer of, 188
Filing Truths, More, 124
Finish lines, 62
Focused time, 139
Forget it, Don't Just File it and, 118
Forgetting, 69
Freedom, Feeling of, 34, 35-36
Frommer's Guides to Mexico, 38

G

Genius at work, 27
Goals, Can You combine, 138
Gotta move around, 70
Group Help, could the Power of a, 204-205
Groups, No, for me, 205

H

Handle Each Piece of Paper once, 80
Hardware, Old, Get Rid of, 184
Have to, 56-59
Help, ask other for, 34, 39
Helpful, 34, 36

HI, 18, 131, 200
Hide, No Place To, 190
History, A Case, 192-193
Home
    Offices, 129-144
    Coming, 178
    Regular Business, 143
How We Feel, 16
Hyperactivity, 69
Hyperfocusing, 69
Ideal schedule,
    day people, 141
    night people, 142

I

If you backslide, don't panic, 105
Important, But what if I throw out
    something, 84
Industry Standard, The, 68
Insights, 61
Internal chatter, 48
Inventory, Let's Do an, 74
Is it relevant, 102
It it outdated, 102
It's about time, 161-167

J

Journalists, 19-20
Jung, C.G., 153, 155
Junkie, adrenaline, 52

K

Keep, papers or e-mails to, 101
Key Concepts, 53, 71, 83, 93, 106, 114,
    129, 145, 161, 169, 179
Kinesthetic, 46, 120

L

Laptop, Your, 175
Learn How You Learn, 42
Learning, 56-59
Less is More, 56
Let's apply this to the Office, 98
Let's Get Started, Okay, 52
Letters, example of how to deal with, 109
Life,
    A Simpler, 51
    Change Your Vocabulary, Change
      Your, 53
Logical, 46
Loner, 205
Long hours, willing to out in, 34, 39

M

Mail, 109-112
    Cutter, Rules that stop, 109-110
Mailing Lists, 112
Make a system and follow it, 81
Making a Decision, 93, 94
    a general guide to, 94
Meditation, 140-156
    is the Next Step, 146
    Primer, 146-148
    Technique, 157-158
Meetings, too many, 199
Memories, selective, 47
Memory
    by association, 119
    Improve your, 18
    Techniques, 24
Movement, Voluntary Simplicity, 51
Myths and solutions, 80-82

N

National Association of Professional
    Organizers, statistics, 108
Neat-freak disease, the, 31-32
Neighbors, Boundaries Make Good, 134
Nelson's Nuggets, 13-14
New Self, put it to work, 159
New York Times, the, 27
Non-filing system, 108

O

Office, Coming Back to the, 178
Optimization, 95
Organized for the Long-Term, 18
Ought to, 56-59

P

Paper, 103, 104
    Clutter, 106
    Clutter and Filing Systems, 107
Paper-Based Filing systems, 117
Paperwork, 197
Passion, your, 196-197
Payoffs, Negative, 51
PDA, 55, 184
*People, The Seven Habits of Highly
    Effective*, 133
Perfectionist, 34, 37
Personal Life and Business Life,
    Conflicts Between, 61
Personal, 75
Picture, Big, 60
Planning, 56-59
    ahead, 123-124
Positive Aspects of the Way We Are, 29, 31
Practical Applications, Let's Put This
    Into, 96-97

Pre-selection, 96
Principles, 151
    Disaster Avoidance, 99
Priorities, no clear, 197
Procrastination,
    ten excuses for, 77-79
Professional Organizer, 8, 210-211
Programs, Old, 185
Project
    system, 121-122
    Company-wide, Make Decluttering
    a, 206
    half-finishing, 52
Pros and Cons, 191
Purchase,
    hardware,questions/things to
        consider, 181
    software, question/things to
        consider, 181

R

Randomization, 96
Reassessment, 203
Rebellion, Spiritual Exercises to Heal,
    148-150
Redundancy System, the, 122
Requires further action, What if it, 111
Research, Just one More Bit of, 135
Results, 45-46
Road Warrior, Go From Road Worrier
    to, 169
Robbins Anthony, 23
Role, the victim, 52

S

Schedule,
    make a, 139
    rigid work, 198

Secret, So What's the, 50
Self-diagnosis, 67
Self-employed, 113
Shadow Self, 18, 85, 153-160
Shadow Grows, 154
Shallow Goals, 27
Sick, Your Building May Be, 189
Sleep, Getting a Good Night's, 176-177
Software,
    financial, 183
    Mapping, 174-175
Solutions, 61
    there are, 70
Something About It, Let's Do Some-
    thing, 156
Spiritual is Practical, 145
Spontaneous, 34, 35
Start times and Finish Times, 136
Strengths and weaknesses, Find out
    your, 75
Stress, 170
    Minimalist, 189-190

T

Talking without thinking, 70
Tasks, difficulty focusing on long-term, 69
Test, 43-44
    I Don't Like to Take, 42
Texas Monthly magazine, 23, 27
The 7 Habits of Highly Effective People, 55
The Last Castle, 53
Things, Why Do WE Do These, 155
Thoreau, Henry David, 15
Three, Rule of, 172-173
Time
    Goes, Do you know Where Your,
        165-167
    is the same for Everyone, 81

to Declutter My Files, I Don't Have
      Time to, 206
Usage Chart, 132
Wasted Table, 137
A different sense of, 46
Final Notes on, 167
It's Decision, 60
Those at the Top Understand, 162
Who Stole My, 130
work takes all my time, 198
Time/Efficiency Addicts, 162
Timelock, 161
Timelock, 38
To-Do
   list, 54, 55
   Doing is Better Than, 53-54
Too Tidy, 22
Tool, Greatest in the World, You've
   Got the, 202
Traits,
   Clutterer, Turn Them into Assets,
      46-50
   Good Use of Our, 34
Trap,
   Free After Rebate, 181-182
   Improves Efficiency, 179
   software, 180-181
Travel, sample checklist, 171
Trust
   your instincts, 95
   Yourself, 104

U

UCLA, 17
Unexpected, Plan on the, 56

V

Value, emotional, 47
Viruses Create Chaos, 183

Visual, 45, 119-120
Visualizations, short, 150-151
Visually oriented, 34, 38

W

Wall Street Journal, the,
Want to, 56-59
We Are Driven, 52
Website, Cluttered, Is Your, 185
Websites, 211-212
What do I do, So if it's not really, really
   important, 99
What Has Worked, 73
What is really important, 27
What You Have Work Better, How To
   Make, 182
What's It Like To Have ADD?, 67
What-If Folder, What about the, 106
Whys, The four, 94
Work, avoid extra, 52

Y

You, Be, 62
Your sense of time, use it to your
   benefit, 163

Z

Zen, 22

About the Author

Mr. Nelson founded Clutterless Recovery Groups Inc., a national non-profit organization that enables people to change their disorganized behavior through peer-based self-help groups. He is on the advisory council of the Self-Help Resource Center of the Mental Health Association of Greater Houston. *Stop Clutter From Stealing Your Life* (Career Press, 2001) was ground-breaking, with its psychological and spiritual approach to overcoming cluttering.

A motivational speaker, seminar leader, spokesman and consultant, he has presented workshops and given keynote addresses in the U.S. and abroad for private industry, government agencies and universities. As spokesman for Mexico's Tourism Ministry, he spearheaded media and public relations campaigns.

His corporate background includes management positions in banking, insurance, publishing, hospital administration and speculative investment consortiums. Entrepreneurial achievements include founding a publishing company, a travel agency, an overseas business-consulting firm, and a self-syndicated international newspaper column. He is frequently quoted in *The Motley Fool*. He is a partner in a wholesale travel agency (Spa World Reservation Service, *www.spagetaway.com*).

Media interviews as an expert on cluttering include: *Dr. Laura Schlessinger, Associated Press, AARP, Joey Reynolds, America Good Morning, Westwood Radio, WLS, Fox-TV, New York, The Debra Duncan Show, (ABC-TV) Houston* and many other TV, radio and print outlets in the U.S. and Canada. *The Houston Chronicle, The Los Angeles Times, CNN,* profiled him for his work with clutterers. International media like The *Wall*

Street Journal, New York Times, Texas Monthly, American Way, Manchester (England) *Guardian* and the *Mexico City News,* profiled him for his understanding of Mexico.

A reformed clutterer, he has discarded more than one-and-a-half tons of clutter from his life. He advises clutterers on the psychological and spiritual aspects of decluttering through a newsletter and Web site, *www.clutterless.org.* About 2,000 clutterers have consulted with him through workshops, meetings, and emails.

A prolific writer, he's published 14 books, many under the pen name of "Mexico" Mike, addressing travel and social issues in Latin America. He is writing a novel.

Born in Las Cruces, New Mexico, in 1950, he grew up in Austin and the Rio Grande Valley of Texas. His adventurous nature drew him explore the Amazon River in a dugout canoe, skydive, scuba dive, spelunk, and fight bulls. He's lived in all over the U.S. and Latin America. Today, he and his dog occupy a 105 year-old cottage on Galveston Island, Texas.

Other Books by Mike Nelson

Stop Clutter From Stealing Your Life

Live Better South of the Border

Spas & Hot Springs of Mexico

More Than a Dozen of Mexico's Hidden Jewels

Mexico's Colonial Heart

Mexico From the Driver's Seat

The Sanborn's Travelog Series (7)

Fishing the Gulf Coast of Mexico